Journey Mystery

Roy Lawrence spent 38 years in parish ministry, during which time he demonstrated how the local church can be an effective centre for the practice of Christian healing. The parish of Prenton, Birkenhead, where he was vicar for 21 years, became a prototype for those wishing to develop this ministry. Since retiring from parish ministry he has become Honorary Consultant of the Acorn Christian Healing Trust to the Churches' Advisers in Healing. He is married to Eira, a chartered physiotherapist. They have two sons and three grandchildren.

To Alison Barr, my editor and friend,
who has encouraged and extended me
as a writer.

Journey into Mystery

ROY LAWRENCE

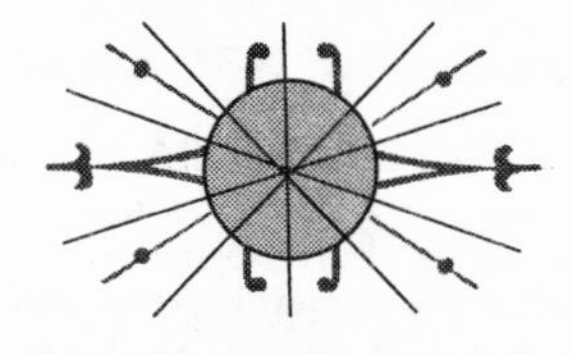

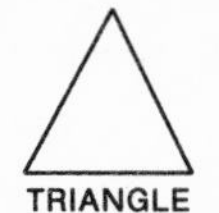

First published in Great Britain in 1999
Triangle
SPCK
Holy Trinity Church
Marylebone Road
London NW1 4DU

British Library Cataloguing-in-Publication Data
A catalogue record for this book is available from the British Library

ISBN 0-281-05197-6

Typeset in Sabon by
Pioneer Associates, Perthshire
Printed in Great Britain by
Caledonian International Ltd, Glasgow

Contents

The stories in this book are all based on real events, but in order to preserve anonymity, most of the names and some of the details have been changed.

Prologue

I Believe in Mystery

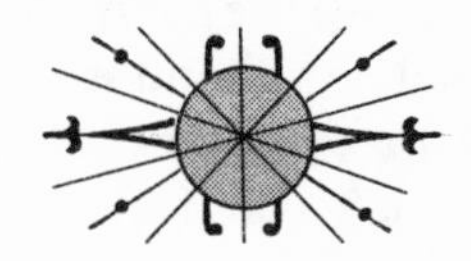

Picture, if you can, an imaginary race of beings who are so restricted in vision that they can perceive no more than two dimensions – just length and breadth.

I think it was C. S. Lewis who first invented the idea of two-dimensional 'Flatlanders'. He spoke about them with tantalizing brevity in a sermon preached many years ago on a Whit Sunday in an Oxford college chapel (Lewis 1949), and I have always been intrigued by his concept and have found myself weaving a fable around it. My fable tells how, though the Flatlanders knew nothing of height or depth, they were none the less on the whole contented with their lot.

Into their world, however, there came a prophet, preaching a strange doctrine of three-dimensionalism. He claimed there could be more to life than length and breadth. He said there was a world beyond the flatlands, a world where there were heights to be scaled and depths to be plumbed.

'Prove it,' they said. 'Draw us a picture. Show us what you mean by height and depth.'

The prophet drew a picture of a skyscraper. They mocked him.

'That's an oblong,' they said. 'We know about oblongs.'

Then he drew a picture of the view one might have when looking down into a deep well.

'That's a circle with another one inside it,' they said. 'We know about circles.'

They began to malign him. Some impugned his motives. In the end they rejected him. They were too scientific, they said, for such nonsense. They had more interesting, more enjoyable things to do, so they turned their minds back to their two-dimensional world and just forgot him.

The fable is only a bit of fantasy of course, but being a vicar in England today can feel a bit like being in the middle of it.

The Church is called to proclaim to the world a message which stretches the human spirit to and beyond its limits. Though we are within time and space, the Christian Church is the recipient and purveyor of a gospel which goes beyond time and space. In the words of St Paul, the Christian commission is to help the world 'to grasp how wide and long and high and deep is the love of Christ, and to know this love that surpasses knowledge' (Ephesians 3.18–19). It is all mysteriously multi-dimensional.

The problem is that it is so easy to miss out on it by being a spiritual flatlander.

We may for instance call ourselves pragmatists, people who 'live in the real world and have no time for philosophy and theology and other fancy notions'. We may say that we believe only in things that you can touch and see and put in the bank. We may see no point in bothering with 'what can't be proved by science'.

Some pragmatists like to think they have 'seen through' religion. What, they ask, is the point in spending hour after hour in church taking part in curious rituals – like Holy Communion? Or in spending hour after hour reading a book as ancient and out of fashion as the Bible? After all, a little bit of bread and a sip of wine, which is often of dubious quality, can't be much of a deal, they say. And they think of the Bible as just made up of words, dusty words from the past.

The trouble is that 'seeing through' religion is just what the spiritual flatlander *never* does. Flatlanders stay on the surface. They regard the whole idea of spiritual depth as an unproved and unnecessary hypothesis. The whole concept of mystery is to them at best a flight of fancy and at worst plain humbug.

They even have allies inside the Christian Church, who collude with them by editing out the mysterious and supernatural from the Christian message, explaining away miracles and discarding whole hunks of the traditional faith, just to make the pragmatic world feel a little bit happier. They offer a flattened out faith, which a flatlander might more easily accept. It doesn't work. Flatlanders are still not interested. The only difference is that now they are right not to be interested, because flattened out religion is truly boring stuff.

Other Christians adopt a more subtle version of flat-landership. They accept elements of mystery within their own faith, but ridicule the mysterious elements in the belief and practice of any Christian group other than their own. So, for instance, people of a High Church persuasion can denigrate Evangelical conversions as shallow emotional experiences, and Low Church folk can condemn Catholic sacramentalism as close to idolatry. Non-Charismatics can regard speaking in tongues as nothing more than gibberish, and Charismatics can write off those who fail to speak in tongues as second-class Christians, incapable of real spirituality.

We can even allow the potentially mysterious elements within our own preferred sort of Christianity to degenerate into little more than formulae. We may trumpet them to the world, but never really allow ourselves to be awed by them. And that is fatal to true faith, because doctrines without a sense of mystery are no more than dogmas.

So, may I nail my colours to the mast and say that I believe in mystery. Mystery is an important biblical word.

Jesus promised his disciples, 'Unto you it is given to know the mystery of the kingdom of God' (Mark 4.11, King James Version), and Paul defined the purpose of his ministry as to 'fearlessly make known the mystery of the gospel' (Ephesians 6.19). To his readers in Corinth he wrote, 'Listen, I tell you a mystery' (1 Corinthians 15.51). In my own small way my object in this book is to do something similar.

Why do I believe in the concept of mystery? I could offer several answers.

One is a negative reason. I am a strictly limited being. I know there are colours which I cannot see with my human eyes. I know that there are sounds I cannot hear with my human ears. It is only logical to suppose that there will be concepts which will be beyond my human mind.

Another more positive reason is that I believe in God. Actually my mind, such as it is, encourages me in that belief for reasons which I will attempt to summarize later. But for now let me once again make what I take to be a logical point – that I cannot believe in God without also believing in mystery. Any 'god' who would fit into my thought processes comfortably, unexcitingly, without challenging or stretching me, would be no God at all.

Then again, what are we to make of the experiences of those people whom we sometimes call 'mystics'? I don't just mean great mystics of the past, such as St John of the Cross or Mother Julian of Norwich, or their biblical predecessors, such as the prophet Ezekiel or St John the Evangelist. There are many folk in our own day whose lives have been touched and changed by mystical experiences.

Let me recommend to you a slender but scholarly little book by psychologist Basil Douglas-Smith, entitled *The Mystics Come to Harley Street* (1983). In it he researches and analyses over fifty statements made by ordinary folk of our own day who have had mystical experiences. You can feel them stretching language as they speak of 'a kind of vision, as if a curtain had opened and I could see beyond – a sense of radiant light and colour and eternity in God's presence', 'a breathtaking sense of the limitless power and certainty of God', 'a feeling of joy, knowledge and unity with all things', and much more beside. They remind me of the man described by St Paul (usually taken to be himself) who 'was caught up to the third heaven' (2 Corinthians 12.2).

If these are neither fools nor frauds, their evidence is a strong pointer to the reality of the mysterious. There is an ancient dictum: 'That must exist, than which nothing greater can be conceived.' It is a hard saying and stretches the mind, but it is well worth pondering. Try thinking about it.

Certainly Basil Douglas-Smith has little doubt about the significance of the experiences he has recorded. He writes: 'The mystical experience is substantially what it claims to be . . . All the evidence goes to show that the mystic is a highly intelligent person who experiences Deity, beyond space and time.'

And he quotes this little poem:

> Don't prattle of 'Religious Mania';
> They're saner than you all – and brainier!

Of course for Christians the greatest mystic of all is Jesus Christ. He not only experienced a deep sense of mystery and spoke of it to others but in a quite unique way he actually *embodies* the greatest mysteries known to humankind. We tend to be afraid of the mystery which he *is* and are tempted to flatten him out a bit, so that he will fit rather more easily into our minds and thoughts. I hope in this book to resist that temptation, as our Christian Mystery Tour begins, as it must, with Jesus himself.

1
The Mystery of Christmas

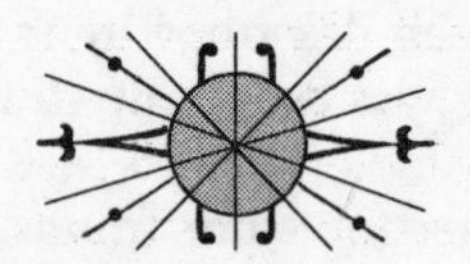

George was the vicar of a large exacting north-country parish. He worked hard and was well respected for his down-to-earth ways and his practical competence.

One year, as Christmas drew near, one of his congregation gave him a warm double-bed-size blanket and asked him to pass it on to someone who might appreciate it as a Christmas present. His thoughts turned to two elderly ladies of modest means, sisters who shared a house and who also shared a bed together. So he parcelled up the blanket, put it in his car and turned up on their front door step. He rang the door bell and prepared to explain what he had on offer.

There was no need for him to say a word. Almost as soon as he rang the bell, the door opened and one of the sisters said, 'Ah Vicar, you'll have brought our new blanket. It's a cold winter and we've been praying for a blanket!'

George was well known for believing in a no-nonsense common-sense sort of Christianity, but he told me he could not avoid a sense of mind-disturbing mystery through all his Christmas services that year.

I was a young curate at the time when he told me the story, but many years later, when I had a large parish of my own, something happened to me which had a similar impact on my own ministry.

You can lose your sense of mystery as a busy vicar at Christmas. There is so much to do that there is hardly a moment to pause and ponder. There are carol services to prepare. There are nativity plays to produce. There are a hundred and one different Christmas activities to organize.

Also, on top of all the usual items in a church's Christmas programme, in our parish we had a large-scale party on Christmas Day itself. We knew that for some people – the elderly, the lonely, the deprived – Christmas Day could be the loneliest day of the year, and we were determined that nobody should feel alone or unloved on the birthday of Jesus. So after the normal sequence of the Christmas Eve Midnight Service, followed by the Christmas morning mixture of Holy Communion and assorted Family Worship, we had a quick break for lunch and then launched into the party. A fleet of cars went out to collect our guests and bring them to the church hall, and there, after a drink or two, we laid on a full-scale Christmas dinner, turkey and all the trimmings, followed by Christmas pudding. Then a group of us cavorted about on the stage in a sort of Christmas cabaret. After a break for mince pies and chocolates, we sang carols for twenty minutes or so, until Father Christmas appeared and gave everybody presents before the fleet of cars took them home again.

It meant a lot to our guests. One of the men, who was something of a misfit in the local community but was a regular at the vicarage, turned up in the middle of the summer and said rather plaintively, 'Only another 180 days to the next Christmas Day party!' And one of our ladies followed up one of the parties with a letter in which she wrote that before her Christmas visit to the church hall she had been feeling deeply depressed and that she believed that sharing Christmas with us had actually prevented her from committing suicide! So though it was a labour-intensive enterprise, we knew it was well worth while.

Miracle of the loaves

One year there was a bakery strike just before Christmas. It was not too bad for the active and able-bodied. They were able to drive around and find a bread queue somewhere. But many of the people who came to our Christmas party were not able to do this, and because they were limited in terms of mobility, health and age they found themselves without any bread in the house. At breakfast at the vicarage on the morning of Christmas Eve one of our sons said, 'Wouldn't it be good if we could give everyone at the party a loaf of bread to take home?' It was a great idea but I had to say that I didn't think it could be done. We would have to find 87 loaves, because we had 87 coming to the party, and you couldn't give bread to some of them unless you gave it to them all. And where could you find 87 loaves on Christmas Eve during a bakery strike?

It would be nice if I could tell you that at this point the whole family prayed about the situation, but we didn't. We just wished we had the loaves to give away. But sometimes God does not stand on the niceties of religious procedure. The wish was enough.

That evening as I was sitting in my study, putting the final touches to my sermon for the midnight service, the telephone rang. It was a local baker who ran a small business which was not involved in the strike. He had been baking bread around the clock and found that on Christmas Eve he had some loaves left over and wondered if I had a use for them.

I told him about our party and that we had been hoping against hope that somehow we could provide a loaf for each of our 87 guests, but that I felt we could not do it for some and not for others. He said he had nothing like 87 available. But then, after taking a few moments to think, he added that he had been taking loaves around to various friends and neighbours, who did not really need them. He offered to have a go at collecting them back again, if they were still available, and said he would phone back later.

Just before the start of the midnight service he did so. I could tell something had happened to him by the change in his voice. He told me that he had driven round to the people to whom he had given loaves and collected the ones that were not needed and then he counted the loaves he had available for us. There were exactly 87!

My own Christmas underwent something of a transformation at this point. It felt as though we had had our own little 'miracle of the loaves' and I could not escape an enhanced sense of mystery at the services that followed. I specially remember the carol singing at the party before the loaves were given out. We were singing 'O little town of Bethlehem' at the time, and I suddenly remembered that Bethlehem is a Hebrew word meaning 'house of Bread'. Our church hall had turned into a house of bread, a mini-Bethlehem.

The local baker never recovered from the experience. He became a regular churchgoer from then on and in time he offered himself for full-time Christian service and became a member of the staff of the Church Army.

It gave the whole congregation something to think about when he told the story later in church. Christian life-experience is often far from explicable. St Paul says as much when he writes that his purpose for his readers is 'that they may be encouraged in heart and united in love, so that they may have the full riches of complete understanding, in order that they may know the mystery of God, namely Christ, in whom are hidden all the treasures of wisdom and knowledge' (Colossians 2.2–3).

The story of Christmas

Christmas is a good starting-point for this journey into mystery. A sense of mystery can be engendered in two ways. Extraordinary events can produce it. But so too can ordinary events, if somehow they become infused with new significance. There are both in the story of Christmas.

Of course it is easy to miss out on this. Christmas can be swamped in sentimentality. It can be commercialized and trivialized. It can be spoiled by family squabbles. It can become little more than an excuse for over-indulgence, a sort of prelude to a hangover, as in the parody of the carol:

Hark the herald-angels sing, 'Alka seltzer is the thing!'
Buy it in and store it away, 'cos you'll feel foul on
  Boxing Day.

But there is no substitute for rediscovering the mystery at the heart of Christmas – and that mystery is so extraordinary that the Christmas blanket and the Christmas loaves pale into total insignificance by comparison. It is the mystery of the nature of the One who came into the world on the first Christmas Day.

We cannot actually be sure of the date of the birthday of Jesus. The early Church was more concerned to celebrate Easter than Christmas, and it was not till 300 years after its foundation that Christians found they had a desire to celebrate Jesus' birth as well as his death and resurrection. It was at this point that Christmas Day was allocated as his 'official birthday'. From our point of view in Britain it was a good choice, because it brought joy and celebration into a rather gloomy part of the year. There was already a pre-Christian festival in existence, complete with holly and mistletoe and yule logs. But Christmas was meant to be more than this and if we want to explore its meaning we need to ponder the one whose birth it celebrates.

As we do so, we find ourselves grappling with the fact that, although Jesus is a solid historical figure, a real man whose birth cannot be doubted,[1] he was certainly no ordinary man. When we read the Gospels we find they make this breathtaking claim. They say that the scrap of humanity who was born in a stable and placed in the feed-box of a donkey on the first Christmas Day was none other than the God of all creation!

St John's Gospel, which is usually regarded as the latest one to have been written and which gives us the benefit of decades of Christian reflection, describes Jesus as 'the true light that gives light to every man' (John 1.9), 'the one and only Son, who came from the Father, full of grace and truth' (John 1.14), God's 'Word' (John 1.1) made 'flesh' (1.14) who is himself 'God the only Son, who is at the Father's side' (1.18).

The earlier Gospels share John's sense of mystery. For Matthew and Luke, who have preserved the well-loved stories about the shepherds from the hills and the strangers from the East, the babe of Bethlehem is 'the Son of the Most High' (Luke 1.32) who has come to be 'God with us' (Matthew 1.23). And Mark, who wrote first of all and was perhaps a scribe for St Peter, names Jesus as the Son of God before he writes another word (Mark 1.1).

Simultaneously Mark tells us of the mission on which the Son of God came to earth. Jesus, he says, is the 'Christ'. This is not a surname inherited from Mary and Joseph but is the Greek translation of the Hebrew word 'Messiah'. In the centuries before the coming of Jesus the Jews could see clearly that there was a great deal wrong with the world. Indeed they had suffered very many wrongs themselves. But because of their conviction that God cares for his people they believed that he would intervene in human history. Someone would come with the power and authority to put things right. When they spoke of him they called him the 'Messiah', which means the one who has been 'anointed' or 'specially appointed'. Their past history was full of prophets, priests and kings. But the 'Messiah' would be greater than a prophet, holier than a priest, mightier than a king. In the first half dozen words of his Gospel, Mark names this Messiah with absolute certainty and authority. It is Jesus.

Matthew, Luke and John give us further information about the messianic mission of Jesus. For Matthew, who wrote his Gospel specially for the Jews, Jesus is the Creator of a New Israel, arising from but completely transcending the old Israel. For Luke, who wrote for everybody, Jesus is a Citizen of the World, the one who can save humankind. For John he is the Cosmic Christ, older and greater than the universe, more mysterious than heaven and earth.

The mystery of a baby

So according to the Bible the startling essence of the message of Christmas is this. The Lord of time has become part of the time-sequence we call human history. The Lord of space has become a 'space-invader' and has occupied the few cubic feet which constitute a human body. And most amazing of all, the Lord of all power has become as helpless as a baby.

What are we to make of such a claim? So far as I know, there is nothing else like it in the religious history of the world. Mohammed, Buddha, Confucius and the other founders of world religions were regarded as inspired teachers and great prophets by their followers, but never as God incarnate!

As we hear this unique claim made for Jesus, Christmas by Christmas, how are we to react? With ridicule, if it is nonsense. With scorn, if it is a lie. But what if it is neither the product of deranged minds nor the ultimate in religious confidence tricks? What if, like the early Christians, we find ourselves discerning the essence of 'grace and truth' in Jesus? What if we see in him 'the glory of the one and only Son, who came from the Father' (John 1.14)?

Then must it not be that our journey into mystery begins here and we have no choice but to fall down on our faces with the shepherds and adore with the angels?

For amazingly it has all been *for us* – for you and

me – and if we accept the Christ who is the essence of Christmas, he will make a difference to us. He will make all the difference in the world, all the difference beyond this world. That is why he came.

Spiritual exercise

May I suggest a spiritual exercise, as we ponder it all? Open any hymn book at the Christmas section and read the words of some Christmas carols. Read them slowly letting the enormity of the claims they make for Jesus sink in.

The old Latin hymn *Adeste Fideles*, known to us as 'O come, all ye faithful', would be a good place to start.

God of God, Light of Light,
Lo, he abhors not the Virgin's womb;
Very God, Begotten, not created;
O come let us adore him,
O come let us adore him,
O come let *us* adore him – Christ the Lord!

Note

1 In *Christ with us* (Scripture Union 1997) I have written of the reasons why, though I am sure that Jesus was a real man who experienced the pains and the joys, the potentials and the limitations of human life two thousand years ago, I am still compelled to believe that in and through Jesus God himself has come to earth.

2
More Christmas Mysteries

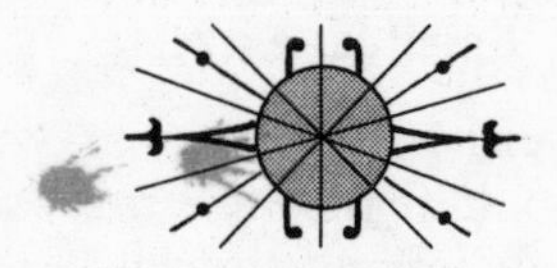

Angels

If the coming of the Christ child who is both God and man is the central mystery of Christmas, it is not the only one.

What, for instance, are we to make of the angels who are said to have appeared to Mary, to Joseph and, in some quantity, to the shepherds?

The Bible teaches that men and women are not the only intelligent beings in the universe. Especially prominent in the scriptures are the angels. There are over a hundred references to them both in the Old Testament and in the New Testament. If we are to think about them in their scriptural context, we have to put aside the popular notion of child-sized cuddly cherubs. In the Bible they are described in two ways. Sometimes they are pictured as huge, fearsome and aflame. To see them is such an awesome experience that those who do so often believe they are in danger of death and need a great deal of reassurance that they need not fear. On other occasions they appear in human form.

In some stories they show themselves in both ways. For example, in the Book of Judges, Chapter 13, an angel appears in human form to tell Manoah and his wife about the birth of their son Samson. Manoah is slower than his wife in suspecting that there is more to this man than meets the eye, but when in due course the angel changes his form and ascends from their altar in a flame, Manoah cries out, 'We are doomed to die!' and it is left to his wife to calm and reassure him.

Earlier, in Judges, Chapter 6, Gideon has a similar experience. When a 'man' who has a message for him turns out to be an angel and disappears in flaming fire, he needs to be reassured by God: 'Peace! Do not be afraid. You are not going to die.'

In both Hebrew and Greek the word for angel means 'messenger'. It is the angel's function to reveal God's will on occasions of particular significance, and if the first Christmas had anything like the cosmic significance suggested in the last chapter, it is no surprise to find that angels are involved as God's interpreters.

The sequence of events is not unlike the stories in the Book of Judges. 'An angel of the Lord appeared to them, and the glory of the Lord shone around them, and they were terrified. But the angel said to them, "Do not be afraid. I bring you good news"' (Luke 2.9–10). Or perhaps we know the story better in the words of the carol:

> 'Fear not,' said he, for mighty dread
> had seized their troubled minds.
> 'Glad tidings of great joy I bring
> to you and all mankind.'

It was the hinge of human history and God's messengers were making sure that God's message came through loud and clear.

According to the Scriptures, message-bearing is not the only function of angels. They are also involved in the mystery of spiritual warfare; they participate in the music, the worship and the festivities of heaven; they sometimes serve as the protectors of humankind in times of danger; and they will have a role on the day of judgement.

We may find it all rather difficult to believe – but it may

surprise you to know that there are many people who are totally convinced that the mysterious ministry of angels has not ceased. During the course of my own life as a vicar several people have told me of encounters with angels. They are ordinary folk whose word one would not normally think of doubting.

For example, I think of Evelyn, who has a responsible job in the media world, and who told me of a motorway journey when conditions suddenly became dangerous and she feared for her safety. By instinct she offered up an instant prayer for protection and as she did so it was as though her eyes were opened to a different mode of perception. There were angels all around her car. She saw them for several seconds and knew that she would be safe from harm – and so she was.

Others have been totally convinced that angels have appeared to them in human guise. Alexander, a full-time Christian worker who lived by faith without a salary, told me of an occasion when standing outside a baby-shop he suddenly felt a sense of shame that he could not make the provision for his wife and child which he could have guaranteed had he been in a paid occupation. Looking at the baby clothes and nappies which were needed he worked out the price in his head. Silently he found himself saying to God, 'Surely you can't expect us to live like this.' It was then that he became aware of a smiling young man standing near him who offered him an envelope. He opened it and found to his amazement it contained the exact sum he had worked out. When he turned round to thank his mysterious benefactor, there was nobody there. To make this strange story even stranger, these things happened in a town through which he just happened to be passing. It was some distance from his home. Nobody else knew he was there.

Or what about Janine, a young wife and mother, who told me of an occasion when for a moment she let go of her baby's pram outside a baker's shop in her home town, only to find that when she looked for it again it had started to roll across a sloping pavement towards the road and into the path of a juggernaut lorry? She screamed, and 'out of nowhere', as she put it, a young man appeared and held the pram. She rushed to the pram and took it into her own hands again. Her baby was fine. She looked about so that she could thank the man who had averted what had seemed to be an unavoidable tragedy but, to use her own words, 'he had vanished into thin air!'

It will come as no surprise to you to read that Alexander and Janine both now firmly believe in angels.

The Magi

But we must leave the angels and turn to another mystery, that of the strange 'magi' who came from the East, bearing gifts for the baby Jesus, and who are such key figures for St Matthew. Their story has gripped the imagination of the Christian Church and in consequence it has grown and developed over the centuries.

St Matthew says nothing about their being kings, but they were widely believed to be so by the third century. Perhaps it was because of Isaiah 49.7: 'Kings will see you and rise up, princes will see and bow down.' Or perhaps Psalm 72.10 had an influence: 'The kings of Tarshish and of distant shores will bring tribute to him, the kings of Sheba and Seba will present him gifts.'

Again the Bible says nothing about there being *three* kings. We have to wait till the fifth century for that. Maybe it was a natural development in view of the fact that there were three gifts, gold, frankincense and myrrh.

The kings did not receive their names – Kaspar, Balthasar and Melchior – till the eighth century, and we have to wait till the fourteenth century to find them presented as varied in race and colour with Kaspar pictured as a Moor. But if for the moment we disregard these later embellishments and forget the conditioning we have received by singing 'We three kings of Orient are', if we go back to St Matthew's account without any trimmings, then who were the original magi supposed to be and what were they doing?

Magi were men of mystery. At best they were mystics, priests or scientists. At worst they were sorcerers or magicians. They represent the fact that this is a mysterious universe, and, as they bow before the infant Christ, Matthew is driving home his conviction that the mysteries of this world can *only* find their true perspective when they are subordinated to the Supreme Mystery of the one who is both God and man.

As the magicians of Pharaoh were compelled to humble themselves before the God of Moses back in Exodus 8.18–19, and Simon the magician was compelled to humble himself before the God of Peter in Acts 8.18–24, so in Matthew's story of the magi – 'they saw the child with his mother Mary, and they bowed down and worshipped him' (Matthew 2.11).

Occult dangers

It is a timely perspective for today with the re-emergence of the occult as a fashionable element in society – as teenagers experiment with ouija boards 'for a laugh', and gullible adults become addicted to horoscope columns in newspapers, and leaders of nations go to professional psychics to be advised about both personal and national affairs, and millions watch 'Mystic Meg' on the TV, and films about occult forces are all the rage.

There is danger here, and Matthew has no doubt that the way to re-establish perspective is to place ourselves with the magi at the feet of Jesus.

Elsewhere (Lawrence, 1998, pp. 74–5) I have written about Franchette and Josephine, two teenagers who came to see me because they had experimented with a ouija board 'for the fun of it', only to find that the result was anything but funny. The ouija board project left Franchette with a consciousness of what she called an 'evil presence'. It was continually with her and caused her a degree of mental and spiritual distress which she found increasingly difficult to bear. It was not till they came with me into church and knelt at the communion rail, acknowledging and claiming the power of Jesus, that the 'presence' was banished.

At a later date there was a virtual re-run of this sequence of events with three other teenagers. The only difference was that on this occasion I was in bed with 'flu and totally out of action, and so my wife Eira had to cope with it. Samantha, one of our local young people, turned up at the vicarage, asking for help. She and her friends had met in a derelict house and found that dabbling with the occult had left them in a seriously disturbed state of mind. When Eira saw how upset Samantha was, she took the crucifix from the wall of my study and the two of them went into church. Again they knelt at the communion rail and Eira prayed that any dangerous forces would be banished by the presence of Christ and that Samantha would be kept free from harm. Within ten minutes the doorbell rang at the vicarage again. Samantha was back, but this time she had her two friends with her. They had decided that they too needed the same treatment. They sensed that somehow it brought power and protection. And they were right.

Kneeling at the feet of Jesus is a strong and safe place to be. In the memorable words of Dick Sheppard, 'The world will be at the feet of those who are themselves at the feet of Jesus' – and that includes the occult world.

Franchette, Josephine and Samantha were, I suppose,

following an instinct, when they were led towards Jesus. But the magi had something more visible to follow – which brings us to our next mystery, the star of Bethlehem.

Stars and signs

It seems that there were a number of unusual phenomena to be seen in the heavens at and around the birth of Jesus. We do not know the precise year of his birth any more than we know his actual birthday. It is usually thought that the division between BC and AD in our calendar has been somewhat miscalculated and that the actual birth of Jesus happened several years earlier.

According to the *Encyclopaedia Britannica*, 'somewhere between 4 and 7 BC is as close as modern research has been able to come in attempting to fix the date of Jesus' birth'. These are interesting years in terms of astronomy. The year 7 BC is particularly so. There are nine planets in our solar system. The two biggest are Saturn and Jupiter. They orbit 400 million miles apart, but if to our eyes they seem to combine, they give the appearance of a particularly bright star. This happened three times in 7 BC. In the ancient world a conjunction of this sort was thought to be a sign of the birth of a king. A triple conjunction would certainly fit well with Matthew's story. At the first appearance of the bright star the magi would note it and ponder its meaning. At the second they would begin to move towards it, consulting King Herod when they could no longer see it. Then, as they journeyed towards Bethlehem, it would appear again.

Whether this is the right explanation or not, Matthew regards the sighting of the star as an event of great significance. Not only were strangers from afar paying homage to the Saviour of the world, but the heavens themselves were acknowledging the Cosmic Christ, whose authority extends far beyond this earth.

The Bible tells us that those who follow him will be invited to share that authority in heaven and earth. This is a concept which takes me so far out of my depth that all I can do is to quote this amazing text from the Revelation of St John: 'To him who overcomes and does my will to the end, I will give authority over the nations . . . just as I have received authority from my Father. I will also give him the morning star' (Revelation 2.26–28).

So it is part of the mystery of Christmas to look into the heavens and to know that it all becomes ours as we become his.

But now let us drop our eyes from the star to the stable. Few settings could be more lowly – yet this too is a place of mystery.

The moments of greatest humility in the life of our Lord were those associated with the crib and the cross. Both were awesome in their own way. St Paul describes Jesus as the one 'who, being in the very nature God, did not consider equality with God something to be grasped, but made himself nothing, taking the very nature of a servant, being made in human likeness. And being found in appearance as a man, he humbled himself and became obedient to death – even death on a cross.' It is not in spite of these acts of humility but *because* of them, says St Paul, that 'God exalted him to the highest place and gave him the name that is above every name, that at the name of Jesus every knee should bow, in heaven and on earth and under the earth, and every tongue confess that Jesus Christ is Lord, to the glory of God the Father' (Philippians 2.6–11).

The animals knew

There is an old tradition that the animals in the stable were somehow aware of the significance of the child in the manger and that at his birth they became silent and in their own way paid him homage.

I used to consider it no more than superstitious nonsense. But then as part of the Christmas programme of our local church we started to include a service at which animals could be brought for a blessing. It happened in my last parish at the request of the children who attended the family services. I have to admit that at first both the churchwardens and I were distinctly apprehensive and that on the morning of Christmas Day we turned up complete with mops, buckets and poop-scoops. We were ready for pandemonium as an array of dogs and cats and other assorted pets were brought into church. But we found that none of this equipment was needed, and though the air was filled with woofs and miaows and other animal noises before the service, as soon as the worship began a quietness came over them all and they remained quiet until the service was over. We thought it might be a fluke, but it happened the same way the next year, and the next, and the next, for as long as we held the services.

The animals loved to be blessed. We laid our hands on them and said, 'God made you. God bless you' – and tails would wag and animals would snuggle up against us. One year one of the dogs came back to the vicarage and scratched at the front door whilst we were having lunch. He would not be satisfied till he had received another blessing, and it seemed that he knew where to come for it, though he had never been to the vicarage before.

I shall never forget the Christmas Day on which one of the dogs got away from his owner and patrolled up and down the aisle during the service till we came to the prayers, but as soon as I said 'Let us pray' – I could hardly believe it – the dog knelt down!

Of course it could have been pure coincidence – as could the 87 loaves and the Christmas blanket and indeed St Matthew's Christmas star. You can never prove the significance of a mystery, any more than you can prove the validity of faith itself. But I believe that life is a poor thing without mystery and faith. Christmas is certainly so.

Spiritual exercise

May I suggest a spiritual exercise? For the moment put this book aside and read Luke 2.1–20 and Matthew 2.1–12. You will find that all the contents of this chapter are there – the angels, the shepherds, the stable, the star, the magi. Read the words slowly, letting them sink into your mind and soul. When you have finished reading, keep silence for a space, with the open Bible before you. Do this on at least four consecutive days. Allow Scripture to do its own work in you. On the first day the words before you may be no more than words. They may not speak to you personally in any way. The same may be true on the second day. But by the third day it may be that you will see little gleams of light and significance in the text, shining into your life. If so they will shine all the brighter on the fourth day, and you will want to continue for a fifth day and beyond, when, if you are fortunate, the Christmas story will be ablaze with personal meaning, lighting the path of your own journey into mystery.

3
The Mystery of Mary

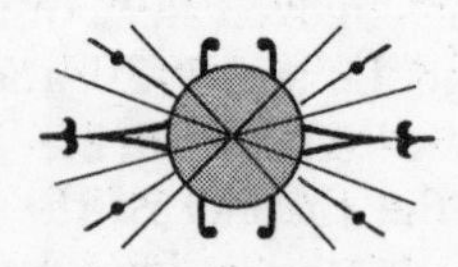

There is a further Christmas mystery, which may not be omitted and which deserves a chapter to itself – or rather to herself. For it concerns the amazing life and calling of the Blessed Virgin Mary.

Perhaps we think we know Mary rather well, if only because so many of us have been present at nativity plays. They seem to be an inevitable part of the Christmas programmes of most schools and churches, and in my time as a vicar I have seen dozens of miniature Marys, demurely veiled in traditional blue, watching equally diminutive Josephs pleading for accommodation at the inn, only to be told that nothing was available but a stable. One of my favourite Marys turned to the congregation at this point in the play with the exasperated comment, 'He really should have booked ahead, you know.' Another looked so appealing that the innkeeper abandoned his script and said 'Come in, you can have the best room!'

However, in Mary's case, familiarity seems to have clouded rather than cleared our perception. For the truth is that the Christian Church has not dealt well with the mother of Jesus. Two extreme attitudes have been adopted to her over the centuries and each has been erroneous in its own way.

On the one hand many have regarded her with an adulation which has bordered on worship. Recently I went to a concert of music from the fourteenth and fifteenth centuries. One of the pieces was by Josquin Desprez, who lived in the middle of this period and was regarded as one of the most gifted and influential composers of his time. It was a setting of these words to Mary:

> I come before thine image, I bow the knee, I plant a kiss and say, 'Hail Mary'. O Lady of glory, queen of joy, mistress of the angels, jewel of maidens and justice of all the saints, consoler of sinners and carer of the sick, recalling the wayward, aiding the desolate, ready in succour – holy maiden Mary. Unto thee, most glorious mistress, that thou mayest keep me in thy care and deliver me from the devil's tricks and wiles and at the final hour of my death may thou be ever at my side. Lead thou my soul unto everlasting joys, where thou, most blessed Mary, abidest in true love with our Lord Jesus Christ, thy sweetest son, for ever and ever. Amen.

The music was lovely, but I am sure the words would have made Mary squirm. She is of course unique among the saints. We owe her more than we can say. However, she was a human being and must never be treated as other than a human being. Mariolatry (the worship of Mary) is a heresy and a dangerous one.

By contrast, other Christians have virtually ignored her. When I started to go to church as a teenager, our parish church was dedicated to St Mary, but she was hardly ever mentioned. It was a low church which never observed its dedication festival and completely disregarded its patron saint. Even as a young and inexperienced churchgoer, I remember thinking how odd and unbalanced this was. I was sure we were missing something.

However, perhaps it is not wishful thinking to see signs of a new sense of proportion in Christendom these days. Perhaps we are now less prone to turn Mary into a battle-field on which different traditions can confront each other.

I hope so, because it is certainly high time to rediscover the real Mary and to stand with a fresh sense of awe before the miracle which transformed her life and which can transform ours too.

Who was Mary?

So what do we know about the remarkable woman whom God chose to be the mother of his son? Actually we know less than we could wish. In Scripture the life of Mary both begins and ends in obscurity.

According to tradition her mother was St Anne, but there is no mention of this in the Bible. We know nothing of her childhood at all. When Mary first appears in the pages of Scripture, she is already old enough to be engaged to be married to Joseph. It seems that both Mary and Joseph belonged to the tribe of Judah and could claim descent from King David (Luke 1.27, 32). We are told that Mary had a sister, also called Mary (John 19.25) and that she was related by marriage to John the Baptist's mother, Elizabeth (Luke 1.36).

There is nothing particularly remarkable in any of this. Mary could easily have lived out of the public eye with never a mention in any history book. Yet this unknown girl was destined to become the most famous woman in the world.

For Mary was to be the mother of Jesus. Her womb was to be God's gateway into the human race. Through her, God was to become man, and as if that were not enough, both St Matthew and St Luke stress that mysteriously her virginity was not impaired by the conception and birth of Jesus. She became pregnant, we are told, as the result of a direct miraculous act of God.

When Mary was told that this was going to happen, her first reaction was one of incredulity, even though the news was brought to her by an angel (Luke 1.34). So if you and

I have to wrestle with any doubts and difficulties here, at any rate we are only feeling as Mary felt!

Soon, however, as far as Mary was concerned, there was no room for doubt. She knew she was a virgin, but she knew from the course of events that she was having a baby. It took Joseph a little longer, and an angelic visitation of his own, before he could bring himself to accept it too.

Many people still have difficulty in accepting the virgin birth of Jesus. For instance a consultant gynaecologist comes to mind, who was confirmed in the Church of England as an adult – but only after both his vicar and his bishop had given him a dispensation to remain silent whilst the rest of the congregation were saying five of the words in the creed, because he just could not bring himself to say 'born of the virgin Mary'.

Not that the concept of virgin birth is unknown to science. If I look it up in the *Encyclopaedia Britannica* under 'Parthenogenesis', which is the name for it that the learned seem to prefer, I find that there is a longish article with 21 cross-references in the index, plus an assortment of references to books and articles elsewhere.

Just to look at the subject for a moment in the cold light of science, parthenogenesis is the normal reproductive method for various lower organisms – like aphids. It is common in others – bees, for example. And it is known in some higher species – such as rabbits and chickens, where it can be induced by a shock.

The theoretical possibility of parthenogenesis cannot be ruled out in human beings, although geneticists with whom I have discussed it have told me that according to present scientific wisdom, if it were to happen, the offspring would be female, not male.

You may feel a sense of shock when I speak of rabbits and chickens in the same breath as the Virgin Mary. But we are commanded to love God with all our mind (Mark

12.30) and it is part of loving God with our mind that we should look at the world and learn its lessons and its laws – because God does not break his own laws.

The meaning of Mary's virginity

So what do we learn when we look at the story of the Blessed Virgin Mary in the light of current scientific knowledge? We learn that, though there are parallels elsewhere in nature, at our present level of understanding the virgin birth of Jesus is inexplicable and unique.

Why then am I able to accept it?

First, though God does not break his own laws, he understands them better than we do and *within* these laws is able to plumb greater depths and employ greater resources than we can. Second, even our own scientific laws are continually being reassessed and redefined in the light of new discoveries. Third, loving God with our minds involves using our minds to the full – but not deifying our minds! There will be times when our minds will be too small to sit astride the mystery of life. Fourth – and perhaps this is most important of all – when we identify those occasions on which we feel we should allow faith to move ahead of intellect, we must be clear why we are doing so, and in the case of the doctrine of the virgin birth of Jesus the reasons are abundantly clear. Think back for a moment to Chapter 1. The whole concept of the incarnation – of God becoming man – is itself unique, unique in the religions of the world, unique in human history. If we can accept the greater miracle of the incarnation, I cannot see that it is necessary to reject the lesser miracle of the virgin birth. When it is reduced to its basic essentials, the heart of this doctrine is that at the very moment of the conception of Jesus, deity and humanity came together – just as they were to remain together throughout the life of Jesus and then in the mystery of his death, resurrection and ascension.

I am able to believe in the virgin birth because I believe in the incarnation (not the other way round), and I guess that St Luke, who was, we believe, a doctor who knew about normal obstetrics, would have said exactly the same thing, had any of his readers asked him.

Handmaid of the Lord

So back to the mystery of Mary – the unknown Jewish girl, into whom God came uniquely that she might become the mother of the saviour of the world.

Her first reaction, as we have seen, was one of incredulity – 'How can this be, since I am a virgin?' (Luke 1.34). But, when the angel assured her that 'nothing is impossible with God' (Luke 1.37), Mary accepted the mystery and offered God her humility and her servanthood – 'I am the Lord's servant. May it be to me as you have said' (Luke 1.38).

She soon found that there was a growing spirit of praise in her heart. This is embodied in the great hymn which St Luke attributes to her, which we know as the Magnificat – 'My soul praises the Lord and my spirit rejoices in God my Saviour' (Luke 1.46–47). After the birth of Jesus she made the whole of her experience a matter for ongoing meditation: 'Mary treasured up all these things and pondered them in her heart' (Luke 2.19).

But she was not permitted to live her life on a spiritual mountain top. She was to experience both the joys and the stresses of life in a steadily growing family. For Jesus was to have both brothers and sisters (Matthew 13.55–56). There were to be days of panic, as when Jesus was lost as a boy amid the crowds of Jerusalem and could not be found till the third day (Luke 2.41–50). We hear no more of Joseph after this event, and so we conclude that he died before Mary and that she had to face years of life as a widow.

The years of widowhood were not free from trouble for her. Both within her neighbourhood and within the family itself the nature and mission of Jesus were misunderstood (Matthew 13.57). There were occasions when she hardly understood Jesus herself (John 2.4). There was the ultimate heartbreak of watching Jesus die on the cross (John 19.25). She must have remembered the strange words spoken to her by the elderly Simeon soon after the birth of Jesus: 'A sword will pierce your own soul too' (Luke 2.35). After the death of Jesus she passed into the care of St John (John 19.27) and a life of prayer (Acts 1.14), but once again of obscurity.

There are various traditions about the rest of her life, but they are unreliable and sometimes contradictory. For instance, according to one of them, John refused to leave Palestine till Mary had died in his arms. According to another they both left Palestine and went to Ephesus together. But if we confine ourselves to the Bible, we leave Mary in the upper room in prayer with the Apostles and other Christians, who now included the brothers of Jesus. She does not appear in Scripture again.

Ordinary *and* extraordinary

So Mary's life is a strange mixture of the totally ordinary and the miraculously extraordinary. Her mysterious significance for us lies in *both*. We diminish her if we disregard either the extraordinary or the ordinary aspects of her story.

Martin Luther had a gift for holding both of these in perfect balance. For instance he preached a sermon on the nativity, which I believe could well be read in every church every Christmas. Here are some extracts from it:

> How unobtrusively and simply do those events take place on earth that are so heralded in heaven! On earth

it happened in this wise: There was a poor young wife, Mary of Nazareth, among the meanest dwellers of the town, so little esteemed that none noticed the great wonder that she carried. She was silent, did not vaunt herself, but served her husband, who had no man nor maid. They simply left the house. Perhaps they had a donkey for Mary to ride upon, though the Gospels say nothing about it, and we may well believe that she went on foot . . . When she arrived there was no room for her! The inn was full. No one would release a room to this pregnant woman. She had to go to a cow stall and there bring forth the Maker of all creatures because nobody would give way . . . No one regarded this young wife bringing forth her first-born. No one took her condition to heart. No one noticed that in a strange place she had not the very least thing needful in child-birth. There she was without preparation: no light, no fire, in the dead of night, in thick darkness. No one came to give the customary assistance. The guests swarming in the inn were carousing, and no one attended to this woman . . . There was no one there to bathe the Baby. No warm water, nor even cold. No fire, no light. The mother was herself the midwife and the maid. The cold manger was the bed and the bathtub.

Then in complete contrast Luther continues:

Behold Christ lying in the lap of his young mother. What can be sweeter than the Babe, what more lovely than the mother! What fairer than her youth! What more gracious than her virginity! Look at the Child, knowing nothing. Yet all that is belongs to him, that your conscience should not fear but take comfort in him. Doubt nothing. To me there is no greater consolation given to mankind than this, that Christ became man, a child, a babe, playing in the lap and at the breasts of his

> most gracious mother. Who is there whom this sight would not comfort? Now is overcome the power of sin, death, hell, conscience and guilt, if you come to this gurgling Babe and believe that he is come, not to judge you, but to save. (Bainton 1955)

Spiritual exercise

These words of Martin Luther can serve as the basis of our next spiritual exercise. If you treat them in much the same way as the carols at the end of Chapter 1, allowing them to sink deeply into you, they can aid your personal journey into mystery. Each time you use them, I suggest that you follow them by slowly reading the words of the Magnificat. If you are used to traditional worship, you may prefer to use the old Prayer Book version: 'My soul doth magnify the Lord and my spirit hath rejoiced in God my Saviour. For he hath regarded the lowliness of his handmaiden.'

The 'doth's and 'hath's are eliminated in more recent prayer books, and modern hymn books contain a well-known version by Timothy Dudley Smith, 'Tell out, my soul, the greatness of the Lord'. Or you can just take whatever version of the Bible you use and read the words in Luke 1.46–55.

When I first became a churchgoer, I used to feel very odd singing the traditional Magnificat and describing myself week by week as a 'hand-maiden'. It did not occur to me that there was a certain justice in it, because the women of the congregation were expected to use male language all the time, and in fact the opening words of the service were 'Dearly beloved brethren'!

Apart from that, it took me some time to see that Mary is a role-model for us all, men and women alike.

The great ones of Christian history have all been Christ-bearers: Stephen, the first martyr, who, like Jesus, forgave his executioners; Francis of Assisi, perhaps the best loved of all saints, who gave his cloak to a beggar and his life to the poor; Father Damien, who lived in a leper colony and finally became a leper himself; the German pastor, Dietrich Bonhoeffer, who died in a Gestapo prison, because he would not renounce or conceal his convictions as a Christian; Martin Luther King who lived and died for the advancement of racial equality in the USA; Mother Teresa, who washed the feet and tended the wounds of the destitute in Calcutta and beyond. These and others like them have brought Jesus into the world afresh. They have shown Christ anew to any who have had eyes to see.

And for our own part you and I have probably encountered those who have made Jesus real to us by the Christ they carried within them. Several come into my mind as I write: a missionary doctor, who spent much of her life offering medical care to Indian women who would not have had it otherwise; a Franciscan brother, who like the founder of his order never seemed to have a decent overcoat, because every time he was given one he gave it away again; a Christian businessman, whose faith shines out both at home and at work, and who has sometimes had to pay a heavy price because this is so; a health visitor, who because she loves our Lord gives her patient much more than medical care and whose heart and home are never closed to any in need. They have been 'Christ-bearers', and as such have followed in the steps of Mary. Scripture invites you and me to follow in those steps too.

Mary is the supreme reminder of the mystery of 'Christ in you', which is not only your personal hope of glory but can become through you the hope of glory for others too.

Listen to St Paul as he speaks of 'the mystery that has been kept hidden for ages and generations, but is disclosed to the saints. To them God has chosen to make known among the Gentiles the glorious riches of this mystery, which is Christ in you, the hope of glory' (Colossians 1.26–27).

In biblical terms every member of the Christian Church can be called a saint. If you are a committed Christian, this text is about *you*.

So, if we are serious about our Christianity, there is a real sense in which the mystery of Mary is meant in some small way to become our mystery too. To learn from and join with Mary in bringing Christ to the world may well involve us in some discomfort. It did for Mary. It may cause something of a revolution within our personal life. It certainly did for Mary. But there can be no greater calling, and as here and now you read these words, the world is waiting for your response.

4
The First and Last Mysteries of Jesus

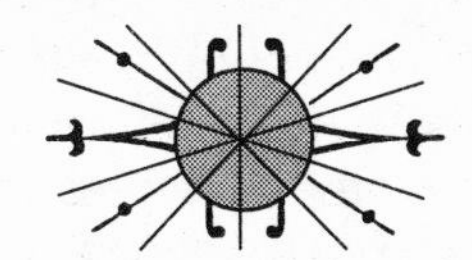

The day before I sat down to write these words I found myself at a conference talking to a doctor who has only recently started to attend church. It was clear that she is well on the way to becoming a committed Christian, but, even so, she told me that though she feels at ease with the concept of God the Father, she still has difficulty with some of the teaching she hears about Jesus.

I think she hoped that I might perhaps soft-pedal that teaching whilst we were in conversation together, but I found I was not able to do that. For it is an integral part of our journey into Christian mystery to be confronted by one extraordinary claim after another about the role and nature of Jesus Christ.

In this chapter we come to two of the most amazing and outrageous claims that any religious faith could possibly make about its founder. These doctrines challenge and stretch our powers of thought and imagination to such an extent that many a preacher finds it easier to say little about them from the pulpit, and a lot of Christians largely ignore them both.

One of them is associated with the dawn of creation. The other looks ahead to the end of time as we know it.

Actually, if the Christian Faith is right in teaching that

Jesus is truly God as well as being fully human, logically we should not be surprised at either of them. But see how you react, as we take a deep breath and then plunge into a consideration of the first and last mysteries of Jesus.

Jesus as Creator

Were you to ask the average Christian, 'Who created the universe?', the answer would probably be 'God the Father'. Yet it would be equally correct to answer 'Jesus'.

Actually we say so again and again, if we worship in church. For instance when we join in the Nicene Creed week by week, we say 'Through him [Jesus] all things were made'. Yet somehow we fail to take it in. We also often fail to absorb the fact that many of the hymns we love to sing also affirm Jesus as creator. Think of the second verse of 'At the name of Jesus':

At his voice creation
Sprang at once to sight,
All the angel faces,
All the hosts of light,
Thrones and Dominations,
Stars upon their way,
All the heavenly orders
In their great array.
(Caroline Noel, 1817–77)

Or there are these words about Jesus from 'Crown him with many crowns':

Crown him the Lord of years,
The Potentate of Time,
Creator of the rolling spheres,
Ineffably sublime.
(Matthew Bridges, 1800–94)

Modern hymns contain the same truth. For instance Graham Kendrick's 'The Servant King' reminds us that the hands nailed to the cross are the same 'Hands that flung stars into space'. Another recent favourite, 'Jesus is Lord!' by David J. Mansell speaks of Jesus as Creator and pictures trees, flowers, sun, moon and stars acknowledging his creatorship.

All of this is firmly based on Scripture. The scriptural doctrine of the first mystery of Jesus is nowhere better expressed than at the beginning of the Gospel according to St John, which takes us back to the moment of creation and shows us Jesus as the heart of it all.

'In the beginning,' writes St John, echoing Genesis Chapter 1, 'was the Word, and the Word was with God and the Word was God' (John 1.1).

As we ask ourselves what this mysterious 'Word' might be, John corrects our question. We should ask not 'What?' but 'Who?' 'Through him all things were made; without him nothing was made that has been made. In him was life, and that life was the light of men' (John 1.3).

As we ask for his name, we are kept in suspense for a while, and the Fourth Gospel continues: 'There was a man who was sent from God: his name was John [the Baptist]' (John 1.6). But he is not the one for whom we are looking (John 1.8).

So the Gospel takes us back to the mysterious 'Creator-Word' and offers us more clues about his identity. 'He was in the world, and though the world was made through him, the world did not recognise him' (John 1.10).

Then suddenly John moves his focus from the moment of creation to his own day and age. 'The Word became flesh and lived for a while among us. We have seen his glory, the glory of the one and only Son, who came from the Father, full of grace and truth' (John 1.14).

Finally he uses John the Baptist to identify the Word, the Creator of the universe, as none other than Jesus (John

1.15–34). He explains that this identification is the whole point and purpose of John the Baptist's life and ministry. It is also the major focus of St John's Gospel.

Much of the New Testament has the same focus. For instance the Epistle to the Colossians says of Jesus: 'By him all things were created: things in heaven and on earth, visible and invisible, whether thrones or powers or rulers or authorities; all things were created by him and for him. He is before all things, and in him all things hold together' (Colossians 1.16–17).

So do we long to understand the nature and purpose of this mysterious universe, but is it all too much for us? Are our minds too small? Is our vision too restricted?

Amazingly the answer has been scaled down for our benefit, miraculously presented to us in totally human terms. In the words of the first letter of St John, 'That which was from the beginning' is none other than that 'which we have heard, which we have seen with our eyes, which we have looked at and our hands have touched' (1 John 1.1).

The answer to the mystery of the nature and source of life is to be found in JESUS.

To turn the same thought the other way round, if we love Jesus, we must logically be committed environmentalists and conservationists, because all that is good and lovely in creation reflects him, and must not be diminished, polluted or exploited for any purpose which is at variance with his will.

Is all of this difficult for us to accept? Do we find it intellectually outlandish? If so, it is good to remind ourselves that this *is* the historic Christian faith, and if we take the Christian faith seriously we should beware of scaling it down in order to accommodate the flatlander within us. Perhaps it is better to be outlandish than flatlandish!

And we have not finished yet. If we believe that Jesus is God the Son, this will not only affect our concept of first things but also of last things. For the world as we know it cannot go on for ever.

Jesus and judgement

The involvement of Jesus in the last days of this world order is a major scriptural theme. There are over two hundred references to it in the New Testament and Jesus often spoke of it himself.

Chapters 24 and 25 of St Matthew's Gospel provide a good example. As he describes those days Jesus promises his followers that his final coming will be public and spectacular. 'For as the lightning comes from the east and flashes to the west, so will be the coming of the Son of Man' (Matthew 24.27). The sinful world will not like it but will not be able to deny it. 'At that time the sign of the Son of Man will appear in the sky, and all the nations of the earth will mourn. They will see the Son of Man coming on the clouds of the sky, with power and great glory' (Matthew 24.30).

It will be a time of divisive judgement for individual human beings: 'Two men will be in the field; one will be taken and the other left. Two women will be grinding with a hand mill; one will be taken and the other left' (Matthew 24.40–41).

It will also be divisive in national terms:

> 'When the Son of Man comes in his glory, and all the angels with him, he will sit on his throne in heavenly glory. All the nations will be gathered before him, and he will separate the people one from another as a shepherd separates the sheep from the goats. He will put the sheep on his right and the goats on his left. Then the King will say to those on his right, "Come, you who are blessed by my Father; take your inheritance, the kingdom prepared for you since the creation of the world."' (Matthew 25.31–34)

Conversely, '"he will say to those on his left, 'Depart from me, you who are cursed, into the eternal fire prepared for the devil and his angels'"' (Matthew 25.41).

The attendant cosmic phenomena, we are told, will be awesome. 'The sun will be darkened, and the moon will not give its light, the stars will fall from the sky, and the heavenly bodies will be shaken' (Matthew 24.29). But the people of God will be safe within the protection of the cosmic Christ. 'He will send his angels with a loud trumpet call, and they will gather his elect from the four winds, from one end of the heavens to the other' (Matthew 24.31). All of these things, and more, are said by Jesus with a sense of total authority. 'Heaven and earth will pass away, but my words will never pass away' (Matthew 24.31).

So how do we react, you and I?

Often we react with an incredulous fearfulness, and because of this preachers and congregations alike 'do a Nelson', put a telescope to a blind eye, and avoid the subject. Alternatively, because of our fearfulness, sometimes we turn it into a sort of joke. In our home we have a little model figure of a man wearing a cloth cap and a fierce expression, carrying sandwich boards with the message 'The end is near' on one side and 'Doom!' on the other side. We have had many a laugh at it, perhaps on the principle that 'those who laugh and turn away put off thinking till next day'.

Yet according to the Bible these fear-based responses are not appropriate for the friends and followers of Jesus. St Paul says that by thinking and speaking about the final coming of Jesus we ought to bring not fearfulness but encouragement and comfort to one another. 'The Lord himself will come down . . . therefore encourage each other with these words' (1 Thessalonians 4.16, 18). The Christian doctrine of last things can provide a welcome counterbalance to many of the more frightening revelations of science today.

Christ is our hope

Never before has the end of the world as we know it been such a clear, cold scientific possibility. We know that there are at least three ways in which it could happen. It could be caused by a gigantic nuclear explosion. We have the power of nuclear overkill. We could devastate our planet many times over – and still have bombs to spare! Or there could be an explosion of disease, perhaps AIDS or something worse, perhaps superbugs which prove totally resistant to treatment. Or there could be an ecological disaster of mammoth proportion. The ozone layer could be destroyed. The planet could be choked to death by pollution. These thoughts have real power to pull us down. They can re-inforce depressive conditions. They can justify self-destructive life-styles.

I remember feeling sad and helpless when a teenage girl, who was throwing away her health and wholeness by a self-destructive life pattern in which she had abandoned any sort of sexual restraint, said to me, 'What does it matter any-way? The way the world's going, none of us will last long!'

On reflection, I saw that for Christians the answer to this sort of negative thought lies in the Christ who will come again. The self-destructiveness of human sin and stupidity will *not* have the last word. Jesus will have it. In fact Jesus will *be* it! In the words of the German theologian, Jürgen Moltmann, 'Christ is our hope because Christ is our future'.

It is good that in the Communion Service we are invited week by week to affirm not only that 'Christ has died' and 'Christ is risen' but also that '*Christ will come again*'.

So in this chapter I invite you to thank God for and to marvel at the mystery of the Christ who will come again.

It is usually known as the doctrine of the *second coming*, but I believe it could be more correctly considered as the *fourth* coming of our time-travelling Lord. His first coming, as we have seen, was at the creation of the universe, when

'Through him all things were made' (John 1.3). His second coming was at the incarnation, when 'The Word became flesh and lived for a while among us' (John 1.14). There was a third coming following his ascension. During the earthly lifetime of Jesus, he accepted the limitations of his human body and was only in one place at a time. This seems also to have been true during the 40 days of Easter. However, before the mist swirled around him on the Mount of Ascension and he was taken from the sight of his disciples, he had this final word for them: 'I will be with you always, to the very end of the age' (Matthew 28.20). The ascension is the festival which celebrates the omnipresence of Jesus among his followers. For all its faults, the Church can be called 'the body of Christ' (1 Corinthians 12.12, 27), because when we meet in his name our object in coming together is to experience and enjoy his presence in our midst, and it is high time that Christians took the promise of that presence much more seriously and literally (Lawrence, 1997, pp. 91–2).

However, God's purposes are as yet far from complete. Though the followers of Jesus can and should claim his presence, it is still clearly possible for sections of society and for individuals within it to exclude him. God's omnipotence, God's righteousness and God's love require a further coming.

So it is a basic Christian conviction that the time-travelling Christ will come again with power and great glory (Matthew 24.30) and will pronounce God's final judgement upon humankind (Matthew 25.31–46), and this time he will be irresistible.

If God is God, his will *must* ultimately be done. In spite of the horrors which have stained human history over the centuries and which still continue to do so, if God is God, then in the long run human sin and folly can be no more than hiccups in the inexorable advance of his kingdom. God's purpose, if he exists, *must* ultimately prevail.

Of course, for those who are determined rebels against God's love and God's law this is a fearsome thought. But for those who seek to be his people – no matter how half-heartedly – the message of this chapter must be good news. It must also have very practical consequences.

We have already considered St Paul's conviction that these thoughts should bring us encouragement. I want now to go further and suggest that they should be a powerful source of Christian healing.

All shall be well

No Christian mystery is such an exclusively heavenly matter as to be irrelevant to life on earth. I believe that *every* Christian mystery, if pondered in sufficient depth, can make a healing difference to the people we are and the lives we lead. This is certainly true of the fourfold coming of Jesus, which we have considered in this chapter.

Because Christians trust Jesus and because we are taught that at his first coming he was involved in the process of creation, it is therefore a basic ingredient of faith for us that the whole of creation is valuable. No matter how we by our sins may warp and defile it, its essence is good (see Genesis 1.10, 12, 18, 21, 25, 31). Creation is on our side, if we will let it be.

If we ourselves become damaged in body, mind or spirit, we can rest in that which we were created to be. There are self-healing mechanisms built into us. We can recognize them and co-operate with them. We know this to be true from experience. A shaving cut usually just heals itself, because that is the way we were made. We also know it for theological reasons, because this is the way the Creator-Christ would inevitably design us. Healing is fundamental to his purposes.

And how do we know that? He proved it when he came again at the incarnation. The life he lived on earth was characterized by one healing after another. To look at this statistically, if we ask what percentage of the people who came to him asking for his ministry of healing were granted it and how many were refused, the answer to the first question is 100 per cent, the answer to the second is 0 per cent. We can hardly open the Gospels without finding a story of healing on the page before us. The will of Jesus was consistently and demonstrably for healing.

We find ourselves yearning that he could still be available – and this is where his third coming through his body, the Church, becomes relevant. We can and should claim his promise, 'Where two or three come together in my name, there am I with them' (Matthew 18.20). Christians have always believed this in theory. The Catholic wing of the Church has stressed the 'real presence' of Jesus at the Eucharist. Evangelicals have spoken of 'coming to Christ' at mission services. It is high time to turn doctrine into expectation. We are called to celebrate his presence *now* and to know it must be a healing presence, because he is 'the same yesterday and today and for ever' (Hebrews 13.8).

Finally, what of his coming at the end of the age to establish the fullness of his Father's kingdom? We have already seen that the expectation of this fourth coming is a powerful antidote to fear, depression and hopelessness and to all the physical, mental and spiritual debility that these bring. But that is not the limit of the healing implications of this doctrine. For if Jesus stands outside time as well as within it (John 8.58), then there must be a sense in which the kingdom he will establish at his final coming *is already a reality*. He bids us recognize this in the prayer which he designed for our use. On the one hand we are to pray 'Thy kingdom come', but on the other hand we are to affirm 'Thine *is* the kingdom!'

In other words we are not only to long for the kingdom but also to *claim* it as an eternal reality, which can be acknowledged and invoked here and now. We should expect it sometimes to break in upon us when we worship and, if this happens, it must be a healing event, because in the famous words of the visionary theologian Hans Küng, 'The Kingdom of God is creation healed.'

Spiritual exercise

Perhaps as a spiritual exercise you may like to ponder these words, as now slowly and thoughtfully you say the Lord's Prayer.

5
The Mystery of the Holy Trinity

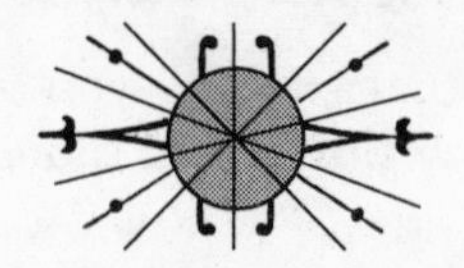

If there is a mystery even greater than the nature and role of Jesus, it is the mind-defying, soul-stretching doctrine of the Holy Trinity.

The extraordinary thing is that many who would regard themselves as ordinary Christians find this a boring doctrine. I used to think so myself. In my early days as a church member Trinity Sunday was one of my least favourite days in the Christian calendar. The sermons seemed convoluted and incomprehensible. None of the metaphors moved or convinced me. For instance I remember being told that God was like water, ice and steam, which are three and yet one. It did not really help and I was glad that Trinity Sunday came along no more than once a year. Judging from the expressions on the faces of many of the other members of the congregation, I was not the only one who felt this way.

I now realize that what we were experiencing was a common psychological phenomenon. The human mind has a habit of switching off if it comes across something it cannot comprehend. We rationalize this process by describing things which are beyond us as 'boring'.

We do it in many different ways. When I was a small boy I was a fan of the *Beano* and *Dandy* comics, but I thought that the *Rover* and *Hotspur*, comics for older boys, were boring because they contained stories rather than strip-cartoons. Later I moved on to both of these and could not wait for them to be published. For a while I still regarded proper books as boring – till *Biggles* and *Just William* burst in upon my world and demolished my prejudice against books too. As time went by I was to discover that there were many fascinating novels and plays to be read, but for a while I confined my interest to books which told a story. Non-story books, like this one for example, struck me as dull. I would not have tried to read one – let alone write one! However, at this point the theological books of C. S. Lewis came along and they not only captured my interest but went a long way towards capturing me, because in due course they were to become a significant element in my call to the ministry.

These days most books are my friends, even some which seem initially difficult – and some have become my very good friends indeed. Boredom, I now realize, is often another word for failure to understand.

There has been a similar journey of discovery for me in terms of music. As a boy I loved the big-band sound of Glenn Miller. I still do. But I have come to appreciate the sound of a great orchestra even more. From bebop to Beethoven is quite a journey, but I am glad to have made it. If I had become fixated in the days when Beethoven seemed boring, what a musical feast I would have missed.

The doctrine of the Holy Trinity may well cause our limited minds to shut down, but it is *not* boring. God is *not* boring. In fact logically, if God exists, the one thing he cannot be is boring. If all the fascinating things in the world were created by him, they can be no more than a pale reflection of the One from whom they derive their fascination.

Evidence of God's existence

The 'if' in that sentence is, of course, a crucial word, but the evidence of life does seem to indicate God's existence. I know we can neither prove nor disprove him. By definition God is too big to wrap him up in a parcel small enough to fit inside the human intellect. But nonetheless there are so many pointers to his existence that even at a purely intellectual level it seems easier to be a theist than an atheist.

In the first place it is our experience that nothing can come from nothing. Everything has its cause. So it is not surprising that over the centuries of human life and thought we have found ourselves searching for a cause for the universe itself. It is a mysterious quest, because that which is able to create time and space and matter and life must somehow transcend them all. And to speak in these terms brings us within a hair's breadth of speaking of God. Creation seems to imply a creator.

In the second place, what are we to make of the evidence of design? If I find a pile of litter beside my house, I shall probably assume it is there by accident. But nobody will assume that the house itself is there by accident. Its design implies a designer. And the universe is certainly more like the house than the litter. Think of the beauty of a rose or the symmetry of a snowflake or the miracle of every human body. Isaac Newton said, 'In the absence of any other proof, the thumb alone would convince me of God's existence.'

Then there is the evidence of conscience, which we shall be considering in the next chapter. Something in us tells us that there is a difference between right and wrong, that the pursuit of goodness and beauty and truth and love is desirable in itself, whereas to destroy, defile or diminish creation and the creatures within it is evil. Where do these convictions come from? If there are moral and spiritual laws, do they not seem to presuppose a Law-giver?

There is also the evidence of the many forms of religious

experience that millions have shared over the centuries. There is the evidence of conversion itself, which we shall be considering later in this book. I know that some write off such experiences as mental aberrations. But surely it is presumptuous to do so – and not very intelligent either. For if Jesus and the saints are all to be written off as sick and deluded, one cannot help asking 'What price sanity?'

There are so many factors which point to the existence of that which is above and beyond us. But it is a long journey from believing in some sort of God to accepting the Christian doctrine of God the Father, God the Son and God the Holy Spirit.

The story of the Holy Trinity

The good news for those who feel more at home with stories and experiences than with abstract concepts is that the discovery of the Holy Trinity is actually a story – a most remarkable one, based on equally remarkable experiences.

The Jews of the Old Testament believed in the God of Israel, with passion and commitment. He had founded their nation through Abraham and the patriarchs. Then through Moses he led them out of slavery and gave them the Law. He taught them about themselves through the worship of the Temple, through the writings of wise men and the utterances of prophets. They believed he was strong, they believed he was righteous, they also believed he was the 'One and only God'.

In the words of Deuteronomy 6.4, his call to them was 'Hear, O Israel: The Lord our God, the Lord is one. Love the Lord your God with all your heart and with all your soul and with all your strength.'

They found it difficult to give this God a name. When Moses asked God for his name, the reply was, 'I am who I am' (Exodus 3.14). But when Jesus came into the world, he brought with him a simple and memorable name for the God of Israel. He taught his followers, 'When you pray, say: "Father"' (Luke 11.2).

So from their earliest days Christians believed in *God the Father*. They did not find this difficult. For there had been many hints of it in the Old Testament. For instance Psalm 103.13 had taught, 'As a father has compassion on his children, so the Lord has compassion on those who fear him.' Probably in the early days they felt that this was a full and sufficient revelation of God's nature and that they could rest in this teaching without too much disturbance of mind and spirit.

However, that was to be far from the case. There were spiritual traumas ahead. All that Jesus did, all that Jesus said and all that Jesus was provoked a major upheaval in their life and belief. For though Jesus was obviously a man, it was impossible to regard him as a *mere* man. Mere men do not claim that they existed before the dawn of Jewish history (John 8.58) and will continue to exist when human history comes to an end (Matthew 28.20). A mere man could not claim that he had come to be the Saviour of the world (Luke 19.10) or that he would come again with great power and glory to be its judge (Mark 13.26). Jesus might have avoided death, had he avoided making that claim to the High Priest (Mark 14.62) – but then a mere man would not have supposed that his death had the power to redeem humankind (Mark 10.45). A mere man would not have claimed to be Son of God, uniquely different from all who had come before him (Mark 12.6), and would not have claimed absolute oneness with God the Father (John 10.30). It would have made it easier if Jesus could have been written off as a madman or a deliberate liar, and those who did not know him tried to do so. But his disciples were unable to come to any such conclusion. They knew that his life, his deeds, his nature were all totally in accord with his words. They had seen him walk on water (Mark 6.49). They had seen him transfigured on a mountain peak (Mark 9.2–10). They had seen his power over sickness and death (Luke 8.40–56). They had seen his power over nature (Mark 4.39). He was not only the Son of God. He was *God the Son*. Perhaps Thomas was the first to acknowledge it (John 20.28), but before long the whole Christian Church followed him (Hebrews 1.1–8).

And there was more spiritual upheaval to come, as the early Christians considered the nature of God. For mysteriously they became more and more aware of God *within themselves*.

The breath of Life

They would probably have known about the strange vision recorded in Chapter 37 of the book of the prophet Ezekiel. In it he finds himself delivering a prophecy in the middle of a valley full of dry bones and, in his own words, 'as I was prophesying, there was a noise, a rattling sound, and the bones came together, bone to bone. I looked, and tendons and flesh appeared on them and skin covered them, but there was no breath in them' (Ezekiel 37.7–8).

The bones had come together, attracted by the word of the Lord, but there was no life in them. However, the prophet was then commanded to call upon the winds from heaven: 'Come from the four winds, O breath, and breathe into these slain, that they may live' (Ezekiel 37.9). As he obeyed the command, the Spirit of God came mysteriously and spectacularly to convert the dead bodies into a living force for God: 'Breath entered them; they came to life and stood up on their feet – a vast army' (Ezekiel 37.10).

It all sounds like a mixture of ancient fantasy-folklore and modern science fiction, but the Israelites were offered an interpretation. Ezekiel reports that God told him the meaning of his vision. The bones represented the people of

Israel (Ezekiel 37.11), who were spiritually dead but by the grace of God could be infused with mysterious new life. The prophet is charged to convey God's promise to his people – 'I will put my Spirit in you and you will live' (Ezekiel 37.14).

For the disciples of Jesus that promise was to become a living experience. There was little life in them after the crucifixion. They were beaten and broken. Their faith and hope were dead and buried with Jesus. Even the resurrection brought bewilderment and confusion rather than new life. We are told 'they worshipped him; but some doubted' (Matthew 28.17), and the earliest manuscripts of St Mark's Gospel end with the words, 'They said nothing to anyone, because they were afraid' (Mark 16.8).

However, for all their feelings of powerlessness and confusion, before Jesus ascended he left them with this promise ringing in their ears, 'You will receive power when the Holy Spirit comes on you' (Acts 1.8). What was meant by this Holy Spirit, foreshadowed by Ezekiel and promised by Jesus? The disciples were soon to find out:

> When the day of Pentecost came, they were all together in one place. Suddenly a sound like the blowing of a violent wind came from heaven and filled the whole house where they were sitting. They saw what seemed to be tongues of fire that separated and came to rest on each of them. All of them were filled with the Holy Spirit. (Acts 2.1–4)

These passages from Ezekiel and Acts sound strange in our ears. What can be the connection between wind from heaven, breath coming into dead bodies, the Spirit of God filling the people of God, and the consequential experience of powerful new life? It would not sound quite as strange to the Hebrew or Greek ear as to ours, because both the Hebrew word *ruach*, used by Ezekiel, and the Greek word *pneuma*, used in Acts, mean 'wind' and 'breath' and 'spirit', and in both languages the words are used as symbols of life. The passages are almost untranslatable in English.

Not that such academic considerations would have troubled the early disciples. They were too busy experiencing it all to bother with intellectual analysis. And with the experience came the compulsion to act as the new people they had now become. These men who had so far hidden themselves from public view suddenly felt impelled to go out into Jerusalem and proclaim their Christian faith among the large international crowd, who had come as pilgrim-visitors at the feast of Pentecost. And at this point a strange day became stranger still. For though the people in the crowd came from many nations and spoke many languages, we are told that mysteriously they could understand what was being said (Acts 2.7–12). Some resisted the disciples' message and contemptuously dismissed it as drunken babbling (Acts 2.13), but 3,000 people were converted to the Christian faith on that day (Acts 2.41).

The Church is born

The Christian Church had been born. Jesus had breathed new life into them and that life was the Holy Spirit (John 20.22). As they went on to experience both the gifts of the Spirit and the fruit of the Spirit, experience itself began to teach them that God was not only to be discerned in the history of Israel and in the life of Jesus but also now within themselves. They found themselves believing not only in God the Father and God the Son but also in *God the Holy Spirit*. They could do no other in view of the upheaval in themselves and, through them, in the world.

Yet they remembered the words of Jesus, 'The Lord our God, the Lord is one' (Mark 12.29). They knew this had to be true. If God is God, then it had to follow that 'God is one and there is no other' (Mark 12.32).

So though it seems crazy mathematics, in the words of the Athanasian Creed, 'The Father is God, the Son is God and the Holy Spirit is God. Yet there are not three Gods but one God.' That was the overwhelming and irresistible experience of Christians in the early days of the first millennium AD.

As we now stand at the threshold of the third millennium AD it remains true, but before we look at the way in which the Holy Trinity is experienced in the world today you may wish to pause for another spiritual exercise, this time one that is Ignatian in its character.

Spiritual exercise

Can you for a time use your imagination to put yourself in the shoes of one of the Apostles? For instance can you imagine yourself to be St Peter on three occasions?

The first is the occasion on which Jesus first taught the disciples to use the Lord's Prayer. You may, for example, like to picture yourself as part of the crowd around Jesus when he delivered the Sermon on the Mount. You have heard him speak about many aspects of Christian living, including the revolutionary concept that we should not only love our friends but our enemies too. 'Pray for those who persecute you,' he says, and then he explains the nature of prayer as an encounter and communion with the God who is 'Our Father in heaven'. It is this encounter which makes Christian living possible. In your imagination picture Jesus as he leads you to put your trust in *God the Father* (Matthew 6.5–15).

The second occasion in this prayer exercise you can select for yourself from any of the instances listed above, in which Jesus showed that though he was man he was not *mere* man. Find yourself discerning Godhead in Christ. In your imagination allow your participation in the life of Jesus to lead you to put your trust in *God the Son.*

Third, read the opening verses of Acts Chapter 2 again. Picture yourself with the other disciples on the day of Pentecost. In your imagination hear the wind of God, experience the fire of the Spirit, go out onto the streets of Jerusalem with the others, wonder at the new life that has come into the Church, and let this experience lead you to put your trust in *God the Holy Spirit*.

But if all of this seems to have happened a long time ago and if you find it difficult to take yourself back 2,000 years to share its origins (because not all of us are naturally suited to Ignatian prayer methods), then read on. For the Holy Trinity is a doctrine for today, a mystery into which we can enter here and now.

6
Backwards through the Trinity

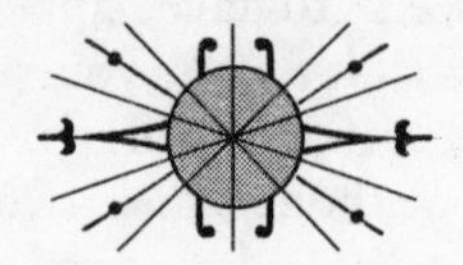

We have seen that when the early Christians came to believe in God the Father, God the Son and God the Holy Spirit, it was because they had no choice. They were caught up in a series of life-changing events, which shook and suffused and transformed them. Later they decided that they must try to put it into words, but, as is usually the case in the New Testament, experience came before doctrine.

I believe that if religion is to be real and mystery is to be meaningful, experience must still come before doctrine. But as far as the Father, the Son and the Holy Spirit are concerned, we now tend to have the trinitarian experience in a different order. We now tend to travel *backwards* through the mystery of the Holy Trinity.

Let me try to explain this conviction.

The limits of relativism

There is in Western society a fashion today for a philosophical theory known as relativism. According to this, all absolute values are to be rejected. One person's viewpoint is as good as another and every human being has the right either to adopt and evolve some form of personal belief or to be altogether an unbeliever. In this process there are no rights and wrongs, no truths and falsehoods, just opinions. The comedian Dave Allen precisely captured the spirit of the age, when at the end of his shows he said, 'May *your* God go with you!'

At first sight relativism may seem attractive. Tolerance becomes the supreme good, narrow-mindedness the ultimate evil. Each person becomes his or her own guru. At crematoria the top of the pops for funeral services is often Frank Sinatra singing 'I did it *my* way'. The theory is that there must be a feel-good factor in society, provided you believe there is no need to feel bad, whatever your beliefs or lack of them, whatever your business ethic or lack of it, whatever your tastes or tastelessness, whatever your sexual preferences, practices and even perversions. If the motto is 'Anything goes', then life must be sweet. That's the theory.

The trouble is that life is *not* sweet these days. Our relativist society is the society of AIDS and drug addiction and death on the roads. It is a society in which there is a real risk that the young will be abused and the old will be mugged. It is a society in which 'do-gooder' has been turned into a term of abuse! 'Duty' has become an unfashionable word. 'Happiness' has become the universal aim – but it is proving a highly elusive goal. Our prisons are full, the Health Service is stretched to breaking-point, half our marriages end in separation or divorce, mental illness abounds, utopia eludes us. Relativism does not actually seem to work. In fact it seems that if you don't stand for something, you'll fall for anything.

Some, however, have become rebels against relativism, feeling that there must be more to life than the hotchpotch of permissiveness which we see in the Western world. In many cases this is more than a negative reaction against the follies and failures of society. It is a positive search for purpose.

Most seekers after purpose and meaning would be surprised to hear their quest described in terms of an encounter with the Holy Spirit, but all yearning for life in depth comes from God and even if it brings us no more than a fleeting glimpse of that which we were meant to be, we cannot be total strangers to the Holy Spirit.

Being alive

It is the work of the Holy Spirit to teach us that life can be lived at various levels and that if we restrict ourselves to that which is shallow and superficial we will not be as 'alive' as we could be.

Not all people are equally alive. In this baffling, beautiful, painful world there are challenges to be faced, mysteries to be acknowledged, depths to be plumbed. It is the work of the Holy Spirit to sharpen our perception and motivate our urge to explore.

This is where Jesus comes in. Since life is as complex as it is and human nature is as confused as it has come to be, solitary explorers are unlikely to make much progress in their search for meaning and purpose. The Holy Spirit himself will lead us to see that we need help and guidance. Humankind has sought this from a myriad of sources ranging from Confucius to Chairman Mao, but it is the Christian conviction that this help can be found pre-eminently and uniquely in Jesus Christ.

I can put it on record as a matter of personal experience after many years of pastoral ministry that I have *never* met anyone who has regretted the trust which he or she has put in Jesus, whereas I have certainly met those who have bitterly regretted their failure to do so. I can also put it on record as a matter of personal experience that I can never be sufficiently grateful for the moment many years ago when as a boy I was moved to kneel down beside my bed and invite Jesus into my own life.

What millions of us have found is that when we trust Jesus amid life's complexities he proves himself a good friend and a sound guide. What Jesus says has the ring of truth and works in practice. And mysteriously we find that he is more than a voice from the past. He is a presence in the present, a companion on the way.

Those who take Christ seriously and put their trust in him gradually find themselves changed by their relationship with him. They find that his life changes people, his death changes people, his resurrection changes people. 'Salvation' becomes more than a word. It becomes an experience, a living reality. It is all part of moving backwards through the Holy Trinity from God the Spirit to God the Son.

And of course you cannot come to know Jesus and remain in ignorance of God the Father. The Father was the ground and goal of his being. He taught continually about the Father. God the Father was all in all to him. If we come to trust Jesus, then sooner or later we shall find ourselves taking God the Father on trust from him. In other words, having moved from the Spirit to the Son, we shall then proceed from the Son to the Father.

In the Spirit, through the Son, to the Father, backwards through the Trinity, this, I believe, is the meaningful sequence of Christian thought and experience for many today who cannot start, as the Israelites of old did, with an automatic belief in God. It enables us to feel our way forwards, doing no violence to conscience or intellect, working at every stage from the known to the unknown.

And it is a cyclical experience. Those who have moved from the Spirit, through the Son, to the Father will find themselves then discovering the Holy Spirit in greater depth and taking extra pleasure in a new awareness of his gifts from the knowledge that it is an old friend who bears them.

Then this in time will take the believer through a deeper

relationship with the Son into a greater knowledge of the Father, and so it will go on and on, mystery following upon mystery, into eternity.

So how about you and me? If the Holy Trinity is not so much an abstract doctrine as a personal encounter, a journey which both takes us out of ourselves to the mystery of the created universe and leads us into ourselves to explore the mystery of inner space – where are you and I on this journey? What is *our* experience of the Spirit, the Son and the Father?

Spiritual exercise

Our spiritual exercise at the end of this chapter can be a time of quiet contemplation, as we allow our thoughts to move either backwards or forwards through the Trinity. And if we need help in doing so, how about these words, originally written in Latin over a thousand years ago?

> Father most holy, merciful and tender;
> Jesus our Saviour, with the Father reigning;
> Spirit all-kindly, Advocate, Defender.
>   Light never waning;
>
> Trinity sacred, Unity unshaken;
> Deity perfect, giving and forgiving;
> Light of the Angels, Life of the forsaken,
>   Hope of all living;
>
> To the all-ruling triune God be glory;
> Highest and greatest, help thou our endeavour;
> We too would praise thee, giving honour worthy,
>   Now and for ever. Amen.

(translated by Percy Dearmer, 1867–1936)

Or there are these words from a hymn that is traditionally ascribed to St Patrick:

I bind unto myself today
The strong name of the Trinity,
By invocation of the same,
The Three in One and One in Three.

I bind unto myself today
The power of God to hold and lead,
His eye to watch, His might to stay,
His ear to hearken to my need.
The wisdom of my God to teach,
His hand to guide, his shield to ward;
The word of God to give me speech,
His heavenly host to be my guard.

Christ be with me, Christ within me,
Christ behind me, Christ before me,
Christ beside me, Christ to win me,
Christ to comfort and restore me,
Christ beneath me, Christ above me,
Christ in quiet, Christ in danger,
Christ in hearts of all that love me,
Christ in mouth of friend and stranger.

I bind unto myself the name,
The strong name of the Trinity;
By invocation of the same.
The Three in One, and One in Three,
Of whom all nature hath creation;
Eternal Father, Spirit, Word:
Praise to the Lord of my salvation,
Salvation is of Christ the Lord.

(translated by C. F. Alexander, 1818–95)

7
The Dark Mystery

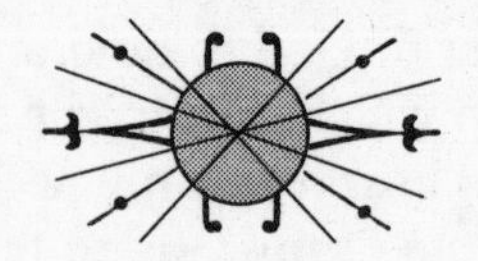

The mysteries of the Christian Faith which we have considered so far have been totally positive in their content – the coming of Jesus as the Light of the world, the glory of the angels who heralded his coming, the lowliness and loveliness of his mother, the amazing claims that Christ was present at the beginning of time as Creator and will be present at its end as Judge, his revelation of God the Creator-Father, his channelling to us and release amongst us of God the Holy Spirit, and, not least, the mystery of his presence with us now.

However, not all the Christian revelations are as positive as this. If Jesus has come to be the Light of the world, then to reject or oppose the truth that is in him is to embrace a darkness which in its own way is also a mystery.

The real world

The bad news which honest students of human nature have to face is that though we are 'fearfully and wonderfully made' (Psalm 139.14), yet we have gone fearfully and dangerously wrong. We are flawed by evil. In a real sense we have become children of the darkness. This is the message of history, where, though we have never ceased to talk peace, we have never ceased to make war. It is also the message of today's current affairs. As I write these words, the papers are full of the horrors of the 'police operation' in Kosovo, there is war between Eritrea and Ethiopia, the Tutsi and Hutu peoples are at each other's throats, the situation in the Holy Land is anything but holy, India and Pakistan have detonated nuclear bombs, there is needless starvation in the south of Sudan, and there have been multiple murders in supposedly peaceful Western countries, some of them committed by children. By the time you read these words, the situation will have changed in some of its details, but I doubt whether it will be radically different in its essence.

In our own British society all ten commandments are broken and their breaking is justified either in terms of freedom required by a permissive society or by commitment to some cause which is thought to make the laws of basic morality become irrelevant. You and I may perhaps congratulate ourselves on coming out well if we compare ourselves with the villains of history. We may be nothing like the Emperor Nero or Adolf Hitler or Pol Pot. We may suppose we are just as good as the next person in our own society and perhaps better than some, but in a world as flawed as ours that does not really constitute much of a claim. How would we feel, I wonder, if a cinema screen were to be lowered in front of a theatre full of our friends and acquaintances and on it was shown a film amalgamating some of the less than wholesome thoughts and actions in our lives so far? And what if our ultimate concern must be not about the judgement of our neighbours but about the judgement of God? What if the one beside whom we must stand for comparison purposes is none other than Jesus himself, if judgement is to be straight and true?

Scripture has no doubt about the answers to these questions. 'If we claim to be without sin, we deceive ourselves and the truth is not in us' (1 John 1.8). Or in the words of St Paul, 'All have sinned and fall short of the glory of God' (Romans 3.23).

It is partly a matter of our own individual choice. As

Susan Howatch continually stresses in her novels, even good people can make bad choices. For instance, in *A Question of Integrity* (1997), the priest-hero Nicholas Darrow is sometimes more demon than saint, and so can even the best of us be on occasion. However, Susan Howatch also stresses that this evil is not only a matter of individual choice. It is often thrust upon us by the personalities we have inherited, the conditioning we have received and the situations in which we find ourselves.

Half a century ago Professor C. E. M. Joad made much the same point as he struggled on his journey from atheism to Christianity. In his book *God and Evil* he described the mental agony he felt at his personal helplessness in the face of evil:

> The simple truth is that one cannot help oneself. To be confronted with a universe which contains evil as an ultimate and ineradicable fact, to know that there is no defence against it save in the strength or rather the weakness of one's own character, no hope of overcoming it save through the efficacy of one's own unaided efforts – this I find to be a position almost intolerably distressing. For one cannot help but know that one's character is *not* strong enough, one's efforts *not* efficacious, at least, that they are not, if unaided. For our burden in the world, as it has become is indeed greater than we can bear, if we have nothing more secure to rely upon than the integrity of our own puny reasons and the wavering uncertainty of our own ethical judgements. (Joad, 1942, pp. 110–11)

Fallen spirits

To compound this problem further, the Bible teaches that evil is not only to be found in our own conditioning, our own heredity and our own current hard-heartedness and wrong-headedness, but that there are other created beings in the universe and that amongst them are some who have embraced evil even more deeply than we have, and who exercise a baleful influence upon our planet.

In contrast to the angels who have chosen to glorify and serve God and whose input into human history is positive and good, there are fallen spirits – Satan and his demonic mafia – who both wish and work many kinds of ill. To pluck one out of the many biblical texts which speak of this mysterious and malevolent realm, 1 Timothy 4.1 warns of the dangers facing those who 'follow deceiving spirits and things taught by demons'.

Some Christians regard the devil and his minions as no more than a figurative and picturesque way of describing the forces of evil. However, there seems no doubt that Jesus took them completely literally, when, for instance, he struggled against Satan in the wilderness in Matthew 4.1–11 and warned his disciples against evil spirits in Luke 11.24–26. So if the Christian Church is right in regarding Jesus as our eternal source of light and wisdom, it is hard to see how we can be free to brush his words aside and to suppose that we know better.

I have written elsewhere at greater length (Lawrence, 1996, ch. 12; 1998, ch. 8) about the sources of the evil which can enter, pervade and use us, and so it is unnecessary to repeat my conclusions here. Also our daily newspapers and daily television programmes can provide better instruction than any book of mine about the shame and sickness of our world, providing our eyes are open to their contents.

The problem of evil

However, there are four things which we need to note at this point about the dark mystery of evil.

The first is that the logical consequence of allowing evil

into ourselves must be self-destructive physically, emotionally and spiritually. In the terse words of St Paul, 'the wages of sin is death' (Romans 6.23). If the Christian faith has rightly identified the essence of God as holiness, purity and love, but the sinful state of humankind has become unholy, impure and unlovely, then we and our Creator have become incompatible. This is a mega-problem and needs to be faced. If our hope of life at its fullest and best is to be found only in union with God and we have cut ourselves off from him, then humankind is in deep trouble.

Second, evil is not *someone else*'s problem. Though you and I may not be numbered among the world's special villains, we have seen, I hope, that we are all tarred by sin's brush to some extent, and it is important in the interest of accuracy and insight that we catch ourselves out, that we actually know about the faults, failings and follies which prevent us from being the people God designed us to be. It is not good policy to model our attitude to ourselves on that of the three monkeys who 'see no evil, hear no evil and speak no evil'. The old Roman sage, Seneca, gave us better advice when he said '*Aliquando te offende*' – 'Be rude to yourself sometimes!' There are many checklists provided by the Bible, if we would test ourselves. The ten commandments and St Paul's description of real love in action in 1 Corinthians 13 provide just two. But we need to be warned in advance. You and I *will* fail the test.

Third, this is a problem with an eternal dimension and an eternal consequence. The biblical term for it is hell. I wish I could edit the concept of hell out of the Bible. I wish I could edit it out of the words of Jesus. But I can't. There seem to be three ingredients in it – self-exclusion from the presence of God, then self-torment as we deny ourselves his life and light, and finally self-destruction since we are incapable of sustaining ourselves without him. Jesus says that *any* other fate would be better than this. 'If your hand causes you to sin, cut it off. It is better for you to enter life maimed than with two hands to go into hell' (Mark 9.43).

My understanding is that hell is not something which God inflicts on us. It is not something which Satan inflicts on us. It is the result of *our own choice*. Here on earth, corporately and individually we can bring a sort of hell upon each other and on ourselves. And in a deeper and more terrible sense we can make hell our destiny in eternity too by using our free will to reject and exclude God from our souls. Let us not deceive ourselves. We are well capable of doing just that. Sin makes us stupid and incredibly it will be our own doing if we set our course for 'the darkness, where there will be weeping and gnashing of teeth' (Matthew 25.30).

If you find this difficult to believe, consider a homely illustration. Think about the common-or-garden attitude of mind which we call 'a grudge'. Grudges do much more harm to those who bear them than to those against whom they are held. Nobody who cherishes a grudge feels happy. They can stop us eating well and sleeping well; they can become such an obsession that they interfere with our efficiency at work and our peace of mind at home; they can make us physically ill. If we have a tendency – say – to arthritis or asthma, we can find that the cherished resentment involved in a grudge can activate these conditions. They can clog us up mentally, so that we are no longer capable of straight thinking, and physically, leading (would you believe it?) to catarrh at one end or constipation at the other, and spiritually, so that all sense of the joy of the Lord is lost. In fact to be the prisoner of a grudge is to experience confinement within a tiny corner of hell. The exercise of forgiveness is the way out of that corner, and yet how often we reject it. How often we cuddle our grudges as though they were precious possessions, jewels and treasures, rather than the poisonous follies which in reality they are. Again and again we choose the mini-hell of resentment rather than the freedom which comes from forgiveness. And that which we do in small matters we are well able to do in larger ones too.

So evil is a problem. It is a serious problem and it is *our* problem. It is a problem which affects life here and now and which has terrible eternal implications.

The Good News

However – and here at last we come to good news – it is a problem that has been dealt with. For the fourth truth we need to know is that at the heart of the Christian gospel there is the claim that Jesus has encountered and defeated evil for us. In order to do so he had himself to experience a dark and unique horror in death upon the cross.

There is no deeper mystery than this in the Christian faith. For if Jesus is God the Son, how can the immortal God die? And why should he? And how can his death be a source of life for us?

Spiritual exercise

These are questions which will require a whole new chapter, but for now to help each one of us ponder the ways in which we ourselves have failed to do and to be so much that God designed us for, here is a short prayer of self examination, which I found many years ago without any indication of authorship. I hope I may be forgiven for including it here. It is a bit like what we used to call a 'creeping barrage' in the Royal Artillery. If it does not get you sooner, it gets you later – and it is particularly suitable for rather respectable people.

Keep me, O Lord,
from the trivial, the interfering and the stupid;
from the infection of irritation and anger over
nothings.

Deliver me and keep me, O my Lord,
from all promptings to decry the person or work of others;
from scorn, sarcasm, petty spite, and whisperings behind the back;
from the dishonest honesty of frankness meant to hurt.
Deliver me and keep me, O my Lord,
from hasty judgements, biassed judgements, cruel judgements, and all pleasure in them;
from resentment over disapproval or reproof, whether just or unjust.
Deliver me and keep me, O my Lord,
from all imposition of my own fads or idiosyncrasies upon others;
from self-justifying, self-excusing and complacency.
From all of this and from much that is even worse –
Deliver me and keep me, O my Lord. Amen.

8
Defying and Defeating the Darkness

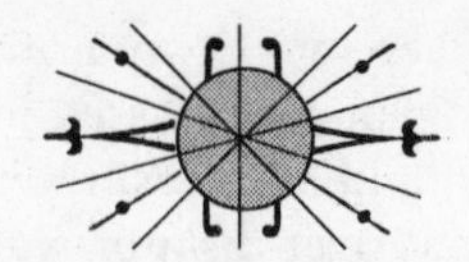

As we come now to consider the cross of Jesus, we are standing on particularly holy ground. This is the heart of the Christian mystery and the heart of the Christian gospel. Without the cross there would be no gospel. It was on the cross that Jesus defied and defeated the darkness that would otherwise have inexorably engulfed our souls and would ultimately have destroyed us.

God's foolishness

The ancient world could not understand it. The notion of God's coming to earth, only to suffer a degrading and humiliating death, was incomprehensible, offensive and ridiculous. Yet the early Christians found that from the cross there came a power and a renewal which was totally life-transforming. That was their actual experience and they could not deny it. St Paul wrote:

> The message of the cross is foolishness to those who are perishing, but to us who are being saved it is the power of God . . . We preach Christ crucified: a stumbling block to Jews and foolishness to Gentiles, but to those whom God has called, both Jews and Greeks, Christ the power of God and the wisdom of God. For

the foolishness of God is wiser than man's wisdom, and the weakness of God is stronger than man's strength. (1 Corinthians 1.18, 23–25)

We must resist the temptation to tidy up the incomprehensibility of the concept of the dying God. We must not seek neat answers to the questions which were posed about the cross at the end of the last chapter. For if you tidy up a mystery, you destroy it.

Yet if we are to follow the command of Jesus to 'love God with all your soul and with all your mind' (Mark 12.30), we must still stretch both our mental and spiritual capacity to and beyond their limit as we approach this central element of our faith.

What the Bible does in order to assist us is to draw pictures in words for us, pictures which can serve as hints, clues and sacraments of truths which would otherwise be too deep for us to ponder at all. It is well worth looking at these biblical pictures and stilling our souls before them, to see if God's Spirit will touch our spirit as we do so.

Some of the pictures are based on the imagery of a law court. Jesus, says St Paul, 'was delivered over to death for our sins' (Romans 4.25). It is as though humankind had committed a crime for which the legally appropriate penalty was capital punishment, but Jesus has taken that penalty in our place – rather in the same way that in Mark Twain's book *The Adventures of Tom Sawyer* Tom takes a beating for Becky.

In the gospel story Barabbas could certainly have felt that way, because he was a rebel and a murderer (Mark 15.7) but the cross which had been prepared for Barabbas was never used for his execution. It was Jesus who hung upon it, whilst Barabbas went free. What was literally true for Barabbas is also true in a very real sense for each one of us. Our sins should have sentenced us to separation from God for ever. God is the essence of righteousness, purity and love. Sin by definition is unrighteous, impure and unlovely. Logically the two cannot go together and yet mysteriously because 'Christ died for our sins' (1 Corinthians 15.3), we have been offered a new and undeserved opportunity for life with God. For many Christians this picture of the Christ who bore our penalty on the cross is the most important one in the Bible.

But there are many others. There is for instance the imagery of the slave-market and the concept that the life of Jesus is the price which buys our freedom. From our point of view at first sight this picture language may seem rather more remote than that of the law court. We know about law courts in our own society. At a personal level I had to be present at several trials whilst I was serving as chaplain to the High Sheriff of Cheshire. Also I enjoy watching legal dramas on the TV. By contrast, though I know that slavery is still a terrible fact in some parts of the world,[1] I do not have any personal experience of slave-markets. We do not have them in our Western society.

However, even in terms of the Western world the idea of slavery is far from meaningless. It provides a graphic parable of the helplessness which characterizes so many lives. Every addiction, every phobia, every obsessional neurosis, every besetting sin is a form of slavery. Slavery is alive and well in England today – slavery to drugs, to alcohol, to pornography, to prejudice, to resentment and hatred, to materialism and greed, to ambition and envy, and to much more besides.

The price of freedom

So when we hear of Christ the Liberator, our ears should prick up and we should find ourselves asking, 'Can the emancipating power of Jesus work for *us*?'

As I ask the question, I believe I know the answer, and it comes as a result of years of pastoral experience in the ministry. I find as I write that there come into my mind the faces of many who are absolutely sure that they have personally been set free in some way by the Crucified One. I think for instance of Gerda, whose husband abandoned her and who found herself enslaved by a dark and debilitating spirit of bitterness for many months afterwards – till quite suddenly it was taken from her in the middle of a Christian healing service. I will always remember her saying over and over again, 'It's gone! It's gone!' Or there was Brenda whose father left home when she was a girl. She and her mother had to fend for themselves and she found herself struggling with a long-lasting legacy of deep and painful feelings of confusion and resentment in herself. But 29 years later she was completely set free as she was anointed and received the laying on of hands at a Christian healing service. Afterwards she could hardly speak for tears of relief. Elsewhere I have told other similar stories (Lawrence, 1998, pp. 68–70).

Jesus said, 'If the Son sets you free, you will be free indeed' (John 8.36). But what a price he had to pay for our freedom! 'Christ Jesus gave *himself* as a ransom for all men' (1 Timothy 3.16). Jesus said it would be so. 'The Son of Man did not come to be served, but to serve, and to give his life as a ransom for many' (Mark 10.45). And mysteriously that was what happened. The price was his life. The price was his death. The price was *himself*.

But to move to another form of imagery, sometimes when the Bible speaks of the death of Jesus, military language is used. Scripture tells us that there is a war on – a war between good and evil. Our lives are spent on a battleground. In fact there is a real sense in which we ourselves *are* the battleground.

The Bible assures us that, in spite of appearances to the contrary, good must prevail in this battle. The fact that the forces of goodness are led by God's own Son is in itself enough to guarantee ultimate victory. But war is a bloody business and Jesus in being at the heart of the battle has been called upon to make the supreme sacrifice. His victory and his death are inseparably linked. 'Having disarmed the powers and authorities, he made a public spectacle of them, triumphing over them *by the cross*' (Colossians 2.15). Jesus had predicted it himself. Mysteriously his triumph and his crucifixion would be one. He said of Satan, 'The prince of this world will be driven out. But I, when I am lifted up from the earth, will draw all men to myself,' and St John explains, 'He said this to show the kind of death he was going to die' (John 12.31–33).

Other imagery is taken from the Temple, where sacrifices were offered for the sins of the world. When John the Baptist proclaimed Jesus as Messiah, he did so by saying, 'Look, the Lamb of God, who takes away the sin of the world' (John 1.29). Paul used the same picture. 'Christ, our Passover lamb, has been sacrificed' (1 Corinthians 5.7). This was particularly meaningful to the early Jewish Christians. They were steeped in the Passover story which told how, when the angel of death visited the houses of the Egyptians, the Israelites were saved because they had smeared their doorposts with the blood of a lamb (Exodus 12.11–13). They were also steeped in the ritual of the Temple, where every morning and evening a lamb was sacrificed for the sins of the people (Exodus 29.38–42). It seemed natural to Jewish Christians to regard these rituals as a foreshadowing of the mystery of the death of Christ.

However, for most of us a very different sort of picture language is more helpful. Many people find it most meaningful when Scripture speaks of the death of Jesus in terms of human relationships, human life, human love. St John tells us, 'This is how we know what love is: Jesus Christ laid down his life for us' (1 John 3.16). Or in the words of Colossians 1.20, God the Father's purpose in allowing the death of his Son was, 'through him to reconcile to himself all things . . . by making peace through his blood, shed on the cross'.

Reconciliation

When humankind turned against its Creator, God's primary aim became one of reconciliation. It was for that purpose that he sent his Son. 'God was reconciling the world to himself in Christ' (2 Corinthians 5.19). But we know that turning bad relationships into good ones does not come cheaply.

I remember learning this as a small boy, when I saw an old-fashioned cowboy film in which two of the characters had fallen out with each other. One had become a lawman. The other was an outlaw. The outlaw was eaten up with resentment, bitterness and selfishness. The lawman eventually managed to change him, but only by suffering a succession of insults and actually accepting an undeserved beating at the other's hands.

Since then I have seen similar things happen not on a cinema screen but in life. Maggie and Minnie come to mind, two elderly ladies who had a long-lasting quarrel. They were ultimately reconciled, but only when one of them was large-hearted enough to go to the other one's door, have it slammed in her face, and yet still to go back again and again until the other relented. Or I think of John who not only saved his marriage to Cherry but also won her over to the Christian faith when, though she had committed adultery, he just went on gently loving her in spite of the pain she had caused him. She is now a key member of her local church and has a sparkling faith of her own. Or there was Mary to whom life brought two sorts of suffering. Physically she was racked by a terminal cancer. Emotionally she was equally racked by the behaviour of her husband, who made no secret of the fact that he did not share her Christian convictions and who sometimes gave the impression of being more concerned about the inconvenience her illness caused him than about the pain she had to bear. However, she went on quietly loving him and ultimately he found her suffering love irresistible. At her death he became a committed Christian.

Maggie and John and Mary and others too (Lawrence, 1996, ch. 2) have all in their own way helped me to understand the reconciling power of the cross, from which Jesus pours out upon us that amazing sacrificial love of his which will never give up but will never hit back.

As we saw in the last chapter, we humans have broken God's laws and have become God's enemies. And yet incredibly he regards us as *beloved* enemies and he has sent his Son to tell us so and show us so. Stupidly, violently, wickedly the sin which is in us lashes out at him, wishing to be rid of him at any price, but amazingly he pays the price.

He dies upon the cross for the love of you and me, and then rises from the dead, still loving us, and still offering to share that life-giving love with us. St Paul can hardly believe it. 'For a good man someone might possibly dare to die,' he writes, 'But God demonstrates his own love for us in this: While we were still *sinners*, Christ died for us' (Romans 5.7–8).

That is the heart of the teaching of the Bible. We are called to a spirit of silent awe as we contemplate it. The imagery and illustrations from law courts, slave-markets, battlefields, religious sacrifices and ordinary human relationships are there to help us as we do so.

Self-sacrifice

Before we end this chapter may I presume to add one more word-picture to the list? It comes not from the Bible but from my own experience. Living, as we do, on the coast, my wife and I are continually aware of the world of air and sea rescue. As I have been writing about the mystery of the death of Jesus, I find that there is one particular true-life rescue story which has never been far from my mind.

It happened many years ago when Eira and I were on holiday in Cornwall and were spending a day relaxing on the beach of a little cove. All around were scenes of typical Cornish coastal beauty. But there were also notices around us warning holidaymakers that this was not a safe place to bathe.

In spite of these warnings one young lad had gone out into the water and swum some distance out to sea. He was soon to find that the notices had not exaggerated the danger. He was trapped by strong currents and was unable to swim back again. The first thing we knew about it was when we saw him threshing about out at sea and heard his cries for help.

Near us was a young man with his wife and children. He put on an emergency lifebelt and he asked a group of us to hold a long rope which was attached to it. Then he swam out to the boy in distress, trusting us to pull the two of them back to shore again.

It was a courageous thing to do and all of us on the beach held our breath as we watched him make his way to the lad in trouble, who was by then in a state of total panic and who snatched at and held on to his rescuer as though his life depended on it – as it did. We pulled them in as quickly as we could, but then realized to our horror that though the boy was alive, the young man who had rescued him was dead.

We tried to pump the water out of his lungs. We tried to give him the kiss of life. So did the paramedics, who arrived in their helicopter soon afterwards. He was taken to the nearest hospital and Eira and I went there with his wife and children. We hoped against hope that somehow resuscitation might be possible, but it was not. He paid the ultimate price for his concern and his courage.

We shall never forget him and neither, I am sure, will the boy whom he rescued. That boy must now be in his late fifties or even his early sixties. I often wonder how he has felt over the years, knowing that he lives his life only because of the heroism of the one who died for him. I cannot now tell you the name of either of them, but I am glad to have this opportunity to write about that act of self-sacrifice and to record my personal lifelong admiration for that man who gave his life for another.

If the Christian doctrine of life after death is true – and I have given my reasons elsewhere (Lawrence, 1997, ch. 10) for my strong belief that it is so – then I like to think of Jesus giving him a very special welcome indeed and of the two of them sharing their experiences.

For Jesus too is a life-saver, and remembering that day on the Cornish coast takes my thoughts to the very heart of the gospel which tells me that it is only because of the One who died for *me* that I have the opportunity here and now of discovering real and abiding life.

So now picture the scene, if you will, on the first Good Friday – the flogged and bleeding body of Jesus nailed to the cross, the crown of thorns rammed on his brow, the pierced hands and feet, the slow agonizing death as he is engulfed by *our* darkness, a darkness which, we are told, actually came physically upon the whole land as he died (Matthew 27.45; Mark 15.33; Luke 23.44).

Amazingly, as Jesus confronted the darkness, he defeated it.

> We may not know, we cannot tell
> What pains he had to bear,
> But we believe it was for us
> He hung and suffered there.
>
> (C. F. Alexander, 1818–95).

In the prophetic words of the book of Isaiah:

> He was despised and rejected by men,
> a man of sorrows and familiar with suffering.
> Like one from whom men hide their faces
> he was despised, and we esteemed him not.
> Surely he took up our infirmities
> and carried our sorrows,
> yet we considered him stricken by God,
> smitten by him, and afflicted.
> But he was pierced for our transgressions,
> he was crushed for our iniquities;
> the punishment that brought us peace was upon him,
> and by his wounds we are healed. (Isaiah 53.3–5)

At the heart of Christian spirituality there is the invitation to ponder this mystery and to clothe it in whatever imagery speaks most powerfully to each one of us. When we have found our own imagery, we must treasure it – but it is important never to disparage the imagery which is precious to another, unless we are absolutely certain that it rests upon some deep and damaging untruth.

Spiritual exercise

If you wish now to meditate upon the love, the holiness and the strange power, which are the mysterious heart of the crucifixion, read and absorb the soul-rending account of the crucifixion in one of the gospels (Matthew, Chapters 26 and 27; Mark, Chapters 14 and 15; Luke, Chapters 22 and 23, or John, Chapters 18 and 19). Do it on several successive days, if you can bear it. Then follow this exercise by slowly reading once again the mysterious words quoted above from the book of the prophet Isaiah, but on this occasion change the word 'our' to the personal possessive pronoun '*my*'. For in the last resort this chapter is not about humankind as a whole, but about your soul and mine.

Note

1 For further information about the millions of people who still endure conditions of literal slavery in the world today as prison workers, child labourers, sex slaves, victims of debt-bondage, chattel slaves, and women in servile marriage contact Anti Slavery International, Thomas Clarkson House, The Stable Yard, Broomgrove Road, London SW9 9TL. Telephone 0171 924 9555.
(Website http//www.charitynet.org/~asi)

9
The Shining Mystery

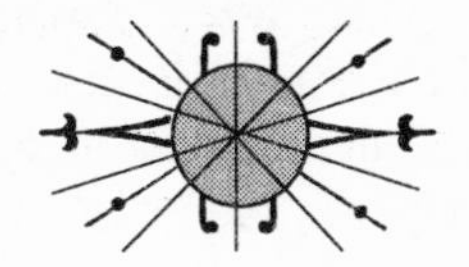

And now for something completely different.

The Rabbis of old had a name for the irradiating light of God's presence. They called it the *Shekinah*. The Bible tells us that Moses saw God's Shekinah in a thorn bush.

> Though the bush was on fire it did not burn up. So Moses thought, 'I will go over and see this strange sight – why the bush does not burn up.' When the Lord saw that he had gone over to look, God called to him from within the bush, 'Moses, Moses!' And Moses said, 'Here I am.' 'Do not come any closer,' God said. 'Take off your sandals, for the place where you are standing is holy ground.' Then he said, 'I am the God of your father, the God of Abraham, the God of Isaac and the God of Jacob.' At this, Moses hid his face, because he was afraid to look at God. (Exodus 3.2–6)

When Rabbi Joshua ben Karha was asked by an enquirer why God spoke to Moses from a thorn bush of all places, he replied, 'God spoke from the thorn bush to teach you that there is no place where the Shekinah is not, not even a thorn bush.'

So Moses learned that anything and anyone could become a vehicle of God's Shekinah, even himself. Later in his life we are told he began to reflect the Shekinah to such an extent that he was actually compelled to veil his face because the Israelites found the divine light which shone from him unbearable.

> When Moses came down from Mount Sinai . . . he was not aware that his face was radiant because he had spoken with the Lord. When Aaron and the Israelites saw Moses, his face was radiant, and they were afraid to come near him. But Moses called to them . . . and . . . he put a veil over his face. (Exodus 34.29–33)

The transfiguration

In a similar way in the New Testament we are told that the disciples were overwhelmed by the Shekinah-glory of Jesus on the occasion of the transfiguration. As St Mark reports it, 'Jesus took Peter, James and John with him and led them up a high mountain, where they were all alone. There he was transfigured before them. His clothes became dazzling white, whiter than anyone in the world could bleach them' (Mark 9.32–3). Or as St Matthew puts it, 'His face shone like the sun, and his clothes became as white as the light' (Matthew 17.2). Or in the startling words of St Luke, 'As he was praying, the appearance of his face changed, and his clothes became as bright as a flash of lightning' (Luke 9.29). To make the experience even more awesome, 'A bright cloud enveloped them, and a voice from the cloud said, "This is my Son, whom I love; with him I am well pleased. Listen to him!"' (Matthew 17.5). The Gospel accounts all tell us how afraid the disciples were. St Matthew says, 'They fell face down to the ground, terrified' (Matthew 17.6). But Jesus reassured them. He 'came and touched them. "Get up," he said. "Do not be afraid"' (17.7), and though they were to say nothing about this experience until after his resurrection, they were to learn from it, and ultimately it would be reflected in their own lives.

But is any of this relevant to you and me? Does it produce any echoes in experience today?

Experiences of light

In Basil Douglas-Smith's book *The Mystics Come to Harley Street* there is still a link between light and mysticism. It is clearly reflected in some of the statements by people of our own day who are prepared to speak of mystical experiences. One writes: 'I was thirty three years old. I had just gone to bed and had relaxed. A golden radiance appeared, and in the centre of this radiance was Christ, as a living presence.' Or in the words of another contributor: 'I was caught up into the very centre of the life of God. It was supremely LIGHT. It was beauty and utter purity. It was Love – such love that I cried out that I needed no other, that never again would I ask for earthly love. I could never again doubt the existence of God' (Douglas-Smith, 1983, pp. 34 and 41).

I cannot claim much in the way of personal experience of this sort, but I do remember very clearly an occasion one Easter, when I had gone into our parish church in Prenton, Birkenhead, to say my prayers and suddenly the whole building seemed full of light and glory. It was totally overwhelming and for the greater part of an hour I was hardly able to move. Admittedly it was a bright sunny morning and the church was ablaze with Easter flowers. So perhaps this was a case of the 'eyes of my spirit' interpreting the beauty around me in symbolic soul-stretching ways. But I could not help going out in due course and virtually dragging the first person I met into church. He was an Irish labourer who happened to be working on a nearby building site. As he walked into church he crossed himself and said 'Glory be to God!' Whether he saw what I saw or whether he was just accommodating an oddly behaving cleric, I shall never know.

Not everyone sees what others see. There was a mysterious incident many years ago when the Revd George Bennett, one of the founding fathers of the rediscovered Ministry of Christian Healing in Britain, came to conduct a mission in my parish of St George's, Hyde. It was memorable for all kinds of reasons, including the immense size of the congregation who attended the healing service at its conclusion. Amongst them was a television crew, because parts of the service were to be shown on ITV. I have written about it on several occasions, but there was one incident in it which I have never allowed myself to record in print till now. During the course of the service there was a point at which a cameraman who was filming George Bennett almost dropped his camera. Afterwards he went around asking the other members of the TV crew, 'Did you see the light shining from him? Did you see it?' Nobody was prepared to admit seeing what he was quite sure he had seen, but the whole crew stayed on for hours after their job was finished, talking, asking questions, drinking endless cups of coffee.

Perhaps similar visions of light are the origin of the 'haloes' which are seen around the heads of saints in traditional art.

If such visions are fairly rare in this world, there seems to be extensive evidence that they are comparatively common at the point of death and not uncommon amongst those who go to the boundary between life and death but are resuscitated.

Back in 1949 a Church Army officer, Captain Edmund Wilbourne, had a brush with death which became quite famous, because though he was declared clinically dead after going into hospital with pneumonia and pleurisy, and though he was moved from his ward to the hospital mortuary, he mysteriously came back to life as prayers were said for his survival. Quite apart from the extraordinary nature of this event (which left a mortuary attendant in a state of severe shock!) the interest which was generated was linked to the fact that he believed he could remember much of his experience between the point at which he was declared dead and that at which he opened his eyes again in the mortuary.

He was persuaded to tell his story in a notable broadcast on BBC Radio Merseyside in 1976, and because of the interest which this generated he then followed it up with another broadcast in the magazine programme *Sunday* on BBC Radio 4. I was writing one of my first books on the Healing Ministry at the time and Captain Wilbourne kindly agreed to see me and answer my questions so that I could include his story in the book (Lawrence, 1979, pp. 92–7). He told me that after various experiences on and beyond this earth he was allowed to have a glimpse of heaven and I well remember his description of it. Heaven, he said, was a place of intense activity, more like a bustling city than a lonely country scene, but the most startling thing about that 'city of God' was the intense light, and in that place of light he described Jesus as 'light itself'.

It began to emerge that others were having similar experiences. Dr George Ritchie also 'died' in hospital from double lobar pneumonia but was medically resuscitated and afterwards was able to tell his own story of venturing into eternity and of encountering Jesus, the 'man made out of light'. He wrote about it in his book *Return from Tomorrow*, but, though he is a highly articulate communicator, words failed him as he described this encounter. He says, 'All the light bulbs in the ward couldn't give off that much light. All the bulbs in the world couldn't! It was impossibly bright; it was like a million welders' lamps all blazing at once' (Ritchie, 1978, p. 48).

Dr Raymond Moody has told many other such stories in his well-known book, *Life after Life* (1976), which he dedicated to Dr George Ritchie. So too has Dr Maurice Rawlings, a specialist in cardiovascular disease, in his book *Beyond Death's Door* (1979), which contains the experiences of patients who have survived clinical death by responding to resuscitation after cardiac arrest. Many of the stories tell of a place of light and a 'being of light', who may or may not be consciously identified with Jesus, though Dr Rawlings also stresses that an edge of death experience is not necessarily blissful and that there can be encounters with a 'being of darkness' as well as a 'being of light'.

But to stay in this chapter with the mystery of Shekinah-light, it may be that we can prepare and train ourselves to see something of it here and now. J. Cameron Peddie is perhaps best known for his book *The Forgotten Talent* (1966) which is rightly held in high regard for its personal exposition of the ministry of Christian Healing, but he is also a man of mysticism and a small group of people have been privileged to hear him share some of his mystical experiences either directly or through a privately produced tape recording. It became his practice to spend an hour or so at the end of each day in a totally dark room, quietly opening himself to the presence of God, and he found in the course of time that as he did so a gentle light began to dispel the darkness. Other mysteries followed the coming of the light, but this is not the place to speak of them.

The limits of experience

James Roose-Evans writes:

> A sensation of light will often come to us in our meditation. Sometimes it will pierce the darkness like a blade, stabbing the heart with love. At other times our whole being will appear to be irradiated, flooded with light,

> and it will feel that we are being lifted up into another region, another time. (Roose-Evans, 1998, p. 119)

'Yet,' he wisely adds, 'we must not seek after such experiences. They are not the reason why we meditate.' And this is perhaps the right point to add two warnings about the subject of this chapter.

The first warning is about perspective and proportion. The purpose of meditation is to practise the presence of God. An awareness of spiritual light may come as a by-product of doing so, but we must always seek the Lord rather than the light, the Presence rather than any by-product of that Presence.

It is a little like the external phenomena which sometimes attend the ministry of Christian healing. There are many of them, ranging from a gentle warmth to something more akin to an electric shock, from uncontrollable joy to uncontrollable tears, from tingling and trembling to collapsing flat on the floor! Much has been written about such things. It is possible to be preoccupied by them. However in my experience they actually have little or no relevance to whether healing is taking place or not. I have seen remarkable healings when there has been a complete absence of external phenomena, and I have seen remarkable phenomena when there has been no evidence of healing afterwards. It is always a mistake to concentrate on the phenomena rather than on the presence of the risen Lord, who is alone the source of Christian healing.

This is true of every spiritual experience. So for all the wonder of the Shekinah phenomenon, we must never seek the light for its own sake.

The second warning is that we must be aware of the existence and the danger of counterfeit light. This is well illustrated by what commonly happens during the mental illness known as paranoia. Initially someone with a paranoid personality will find life elusive, threatening, confusing and painful. There may be some chance of effective therapy at this stage, but if the paranoia is allowed to take its course, there comes a point of no return, and that point is characterized by false illumination. This is how Dr Frank Lake describes it in his magisterial work *Clinical Theology*:

> A sudden breakthrough of 'illumination' convinces him that there is nothing confusing about it any more. It is all absolutely clear and structured. At whatever point in the progress of the illness this breakthrough to pseudo-illumination occurs it is very characteristic, and once it has occurred it is difficult for the patient to retreat from it. He is surrounded by a 'pseudo-community' of persecutors. (Lake, 1966, p. 1010)

From this point he is a danger to society and to himself and psychopathic violence becomes more and more of a possibility.

Something similar can happen at a national level. In the development of Hitler's Third Reich there was no more sinister moment than that when his followers accepted the pseudo-illumination of anti-semitism. Suddenly it all seemed clear to them. The ills of their nation and of the world as a whole could be attributed to the malevolence and machinations of the Jews. Those who allowed this false light to flood into their souls were thenceforth flawed and blinded by it, and in consequence six million Jews died in concentration camps and the world was brought to the brink of disaster. The faces of those who took part in Hitler's massive rallies positively shone. We can see it in old films. But the shining was destructive and devilish – literally so. For as Scripture reminds us, Satan himself can masquerade as an angel of light (2 Corinthians 11.14).

Spiritual exercise

We need to be very careful about our sources of 'illumination'. And so before ending this chapter we must allow Scripture to take us back to the centre point of the true Shining Mystery.

Here as the basis for a contemplative spiritual exercise are three quotations from the Bible to read and absorb.

The first is from the Old Testament and refers to God's calling to Israel:

> 'Arise shine, for your light has come, and the glory of the Lord rises upon you. See, darkness covers the earth and thick darkness is over the peoples, but the Lord rises upon you and his glory appears over you.' (Isaiah 60.1–2)

The second speaks of Christians as those who are called to live both in and by the light of God:

> 'For God, who said, "Let light shine out of darkness," made his light shine in our hearts to give us the light of the knowledge of the glory of God in the face of Christ.' (2 Corinthians 4.6)

And the third – incredibly – looks forward to an eternal destiny in which we are called not only to reflect God's Shining Mystery but actually *to become one with it*:

> 'We, who with unveiled faces all reflect the Lord's glory, are being transformed into his likeness with ever-increasing glory, which comes from the Lord, who is the Spirit.' (2 Corinthians 3.18)

I wonder how many TV viewers who voted Graham Kendrick's (1987) 'Shine, Jesus, shine' into the BBC top ten songs of praise know that it is a meditation on these words of St Paul about Jesus as Shekinah-light of the world, and that they are actually praying for personal incorporation into that mystery when they chorus 'Shine on me, shine on me!'

10
The Mystery of New Birth

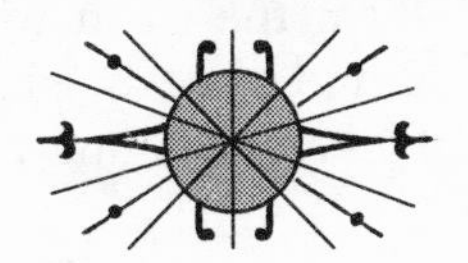

So far in this survey of Christian mysteries our mode of operation has mainly been that of looking outwards. We have sought to do this both in terms of time and space.

The cosmos is deeply mysterious. Only a few days before writing this chapter I paid a visit to the Liverpool Planetarium and came away with my mind reeling. The universe is so vast and I am so small.

And yet it is not only when we look outwards that a sense of mystery can come upon us. It can also come when we look inwards. There are mysteries within the microcosm of the human body, mind and spirit as well as within the macrocosm of the universe.

The wonder of human being

So consider for a few moments the wonder of *you*. Start by thinking about yourself at a purely physical level. Look at your hand and your arm, the hand and arm with which you will soon turn the page of this book. A robotic arm controlled by a computer pales into insignificance compared to a human arm controlled by the human brain. Every tiny physical action you take is in itself a marvel.

The more science teaches us about ourselves, the more awesome we seem to be. One of the great discoveries within my own lifetime has been that of DNA (deoxyribonucleic acid). My genes and your genes are stored in our

DNA, and what an extraordinary storehouse it has proved to be. In Michael Mayne's excellent book *This Sunrise of Wonder* he writes: 'The DNA is so narrow and compacted that all your genes in each of your body's total cells would fit into an ice cube; yet if unwound and joined together they would stretch from the earth to the sun and back more than four hundred times' (Mayne, 1995, p. 99). The wonders of the Planetarium and of my own body are perhaps not so different!

But there is much more to you and me than our bodies. My body can be subjected to chemical analysis – but when that analysis is complete it will not account for the fact that I can compose and play a tune on the piano, feel a sense of right and wrong, enjoy a joke, stand in awe before the beauties of nature, love my wife, and even try to write a book about the mystery of God. For such things I need my mind, and indeed I need more than my mind. For I also need to draw upon that mysterious spiritual essence which constitutes the core of my being.

We are body-mind-and-spirit entities, you and I. The Bible goes as far as to say that this means we have been created in the image of God.

> So God created man
>   in his own image,
> in the image of God
>   he created him;
> male and female
>   he created them. (Genesis 1.27)

So pause for a while and ponder the miracle which you are – the miracle of your body, the miracle of your mind, the miracle of your spirit.

Try making a list of some of your personal aptitudes – perhaps the fact that you are good at crosswords, or have a talent for woodwork, or can arrange flowers, or coach a local football team, or bake a good cake. Realize that nobody is quite the same as you. When God made you, he broke the mould afterwards. You are a unique miracle of God's creative power. You are special, because all miracles are special.

A flawed miracle

However, you are a flawed miracle. So am I. So is every other human being who shares planet earth with us. It is easy to see the flaws of many of the people around us. In fact it is easy to see the presence of evil in the world around us. Sometimes it is spectacular and horrendous. Only a few days before I wrote these words the newspapers were full of what *The Times* called the 'Massacre of the Innocents' at Omagh. Twenty-nine people are dead because of it and hundreds are injured or bereaved.

There is a temptation to think that such dark deeds are absolutely nothing to do with people like you and me, but, as we saw in Chapter 7, these blooms of evil have their roots in that darkness which can be found to a greater or lesser extent in *every* human soul.

The book of Genesis is very realistic. After speaking of our creation in the image of God, it then goes on to tell in memorable picture language of the way in which we have chosen to mar that image.

Adam (Hebrew for 'mankind') loses his place in the Garden of Eden (Hebrew for 'delight') by choosing to put his own selfish desires before God's wisdom and God's law. In the Genesis story the choice is symbolized by eating fruit that had been forbidden by God. Since Adam had been made in the image of God, the temptation was to play at *being* God. 'Be like God,' said the serpent (Genesis 3.4) – put self at the centre of life, where God should be. It was to be a catastrophic and destructive mistake. All sorts of ills were to follow from it. But the prospect of a god-like self-centredness seemed so attractive. The temptation was so strong. Adam fell for it. We still do. When you and I look inside ourselves, if we are honest, we see the darkness of our self-centredness as well as the light of God's purpose.

To recapitulate Chapter 7, we are 'fearfully and wonderfully made' (Psalm 139.14), but have gone fearsomely and dangerously wrong. We are flawed by our own folly and even the best of us have to wrestle with its consequences. The warning of Scripture rings in our ears: 'The wages of sin is death' (Romans 6.23). The evil that is within us has terrible implications, both in terms of life here and now and also in terms of our eternal destiny.

That is the enigma of human nature. On the one hand there is our God-given potential. On the other hand there is our deadly self-induced predicament.

The story of Nicodemus

The gospel tells us that it was to resolve this enigma that Jesus came into the world. We have seen in Chapter 8 that through the self-giving of Jesus upon the cross the deadliness of sin has itself received a death-blow. 'The wages of sin is death, but the gift of God is eternal life in Christ Jesus our Lord.' Sin's power to separate us from our God and our neighbour and our true self need no longer have the last word. Through Jesus Christ and the price that he has paid upon the cross we may have a new relationship with God.

But if we accept that relationship, then what? Christianity is a 'so-what?' religion. Every Christian doctrine has a practical consequence. So what is the consequence of allowing Jesus to re-establish our relationship with God as our Father?

Go back in your imagination to an incident recorded by St John, when Jesus was visited by an eminent Jewish religious leader in the dead of night. John tells the story in Chapter 3 of his Gospel.

The name of the visitor was Nicodemus. He was a prominent Pharisee and a member of the Jewish ruling council. He probably came by night because Jesus was not acceptable in respectable circles at that time and a visit under the cover of darkness was less likely to be noticed.

As a cultured man he began the conversation with a conventional compliment. 'Rabbi, we know you are a teacher who has come from God. For no-one could perform the miraculous signs you are doing if God were not with him' (verse 2). But Jesus would have nothing to do with such polite preliminaries. He cut through the compliments with uncompromising words: 'Unless a man is born again, he cannot see the Kingdom of God' (verse 3).

Nicodemus was nonplussed. Maybe his response was a feeble attempt at a joke. 'How can a man be born when he is old? . . . Surely he cannot enter a second time into his mother's womb to be born!' (verse 4).

The answer of Jesus was that no-one can enter the kingdom of God unless he is born of water and the Spirit (verse 5). Spiritual birth is in some ways like physical birth. When a baby is born, the waters of the womb break and the child emerges to take a first breath. Water and breath are involved in spiritual birth too. The water is the water of life, and St John takes up this theme in his next chapter, when he tells how Jesus met a woman at a well in a town called Sychar. And as for the breath of new birth, this, says Jesus, is the wind of the Holy Spirit. As we have seen, 'breath', 'wind' and 'spirit' are all translations of the same word in Greek and Hebrew, and there would be more teaching about the Holy Spirit as the ministry of Jesus developed (as in John 15).

At this stage Nicodemus could not understand what Jesus was saying to him. But clearly he knew it was of real significance, and the account in St John, Chapter 3, leaves the two of them talking into the night. Ultimately none of their conversation was wasted, because in due course Nicodemus became one of Jesus' new men. When the chief priests and their henchmen increasingly turned against Jesus, Nicodemus found the courage to speak out against their bigotry and their plans for a judicial execution (John 7.50). After the crucifixion he helped Joseph of Arimathea to bury the body of Jesus (John 19.39). And if tradition is to be believed, after the resurrection he became a full disciple and was baptized by Peter and John. We can imagine the words of Jesus about being 'born of water and of the Spirit' re-echoing in his mind as he experienced baptism.

New birth

But what about ourselves? What do we make of the conversation of Jesus and Nicodemus, as St John records it, and of the strange concept of new birth, which it contains?

May I offer three comments and a warning?

The first comment is that, as is so often the case in the Christian faith, if we take it as it stands and resist the temptation to dilute it, this imagery leads us once again into the realm of mystery. Jesus says as much to Nicodemus. 'The wind blows wherever it pleases. You hear its sound, but you cannot tell where it comes from or where it is going. So it is with everyone born of the Spirit' (John 3.8).

Secondly, the concept of new birth should be a humbling one. I had very little to do with my own physical birth. God created me. My father begat me. My mother conceived me. I was carried in my mother's womb for nine months till our family doctor delivered me. All I contributed was a few yelps when I started to breathe.

So it is with my spiritual birth. It is not forced upon me, because God respects my free will and waits for my consent. But it is certainly not my doing. In a real sense all

I have contributed to my salvation is the sinfulness which made it necessary!

Thirdly, new birth is a concept which speaks of unique and radical change. Those who become real Christians can never be the same again. In the words of St Paul, 'If anyone is in Christ, he is a new creation' (2 Corinthians 5.17). The Bible teaches that Jesus makes a life-transforming impact on those who put their trust in him.

So to my warning. If we take the doctrine of new birth seriously, we must be on our guard against anything that trivializes Christian life and experience. This means we must be on our guard against those forms of religion which give us a thrill, a buzz, a moment of excitement, a feeling of temporary well-being, but make no difference in the depth of our being. Beware of religious experiences which are no more than a 'trip'.

The problem with 'trips'

We like trips. Some of us like them too much. We can seek them through drugs. We can seek them through alcohol. We can seek them through rhythmic music with a heavy hypnotic beat. Some people find highly individualistic ways of inducing trips. Vincent comes to mind, a respected highly placed professional man, who likes to sit in a darkened room listening to Wagner, with his excellent sound system turned up high, whilst he has a 'high' of his own. Or there is Elvira, a young woman who told me she had discovered what for her was virtually a magic word. It seemed to belong to no language, but she would sit cross-legged repeating her word over and over again, as it helped her to become hypnotically oblivious to the world.

Escape is the name of the trip-game. It is the nature of a trip that it takes you out of the real world and into a different state of being for a while – whether you are away with heroin or away with heavy metal, away with vodka or away with the Valkyries.

My warning in this chapter is that some people can downgrade religion into a sort of trip. Some go for a delicate High Church trip in the world of ritual and chants and incense. Others experience their trip at a much lower level in the churchmanship scale in the world of emotional preaching and happy-clappy music. And just in case the more intellectual begin to feel a little superior at this stage, it is worth noting that religion can become the basis for an academic trip. It can be relegated to a purely cerebral activity – a bit like that of Milton's devils, who sat on a rock and discussed theology!

Though an occasional escapist activity does no harm and can help us unwind and relax, it is not good to plan life around regular trips. A trip brings no insight into the realities of life. It makes no difference and brings no challenge or motivation, except the urge to go for more trips. True religion is the opposite to a trip because it reaches deeply into us and makes such a radical difference to us and through us that we need terms like new birth and new creation to describe its life-changing effect.

So what is the nature of the radical change involved in being a born-again Christian? For all the mystery of the concept of new birth, if you and I are serious followers of Jesus, we should be able to attempt an answer to that question, because it should be an integral and fundamental ingredient of Christian experience. As St Paul says, both to members of the early church and to us, 'You have taken off your old self with its practices and have put on the new self, which is being renewed in knowledge in the image of its Creator' (Colossians 3.9–10).

So, if we may venture for a moment onto the holiest ground in your soul and mine, what is the essence of this new self, this new being, which is the personal gift of Jesus Christ? It is no less than his own life flowing into us and through us. St Paul calls it 'the glorious mystery', 'Christ in you, the hope of glory' (Colossians 1.27).

Spiritual exercise

As this chapter comes to an end, I invite you to ponder this mystery, this calling, this gift, by meditating upon a remarkable and thought-provoking poem by Jane Clark.[1]

Miracle Births

We are called to bear
The life of the Son of God.
Mary was the first to do it.
An angel visited her.
Believing he came from God
Bringing Blessing,
She said, 'Yes God,
Let it be to me just as you say,
I'm the Lord's maid, ready to serve.'
It was God's wish
To have many Sons.

So the Holy Ghost overshadowed her,
With creative Word power,
And the Son of God became also
Son of Man, growing in her
Day by day until He came
Into the world revealing the
Fullness of the Father's love.
A flesh and blood Son of God.
Because of Mary's yes.
It was God's wish
To have many Sons.

He grew, a perfect Man
Through all his earthly days
Perfected through suffering
Laying down his life
Taking our punishment on Him
Separated from His Father,
So that we too reconciled, could call
God Abba, Father.
It was God's wish
To have many Sons.

God visited me like Mary,
As I said yes to Him
The Holy Ghost overshadowed me
With creative Word power;
The Son of God is born in me
Growing in me day by day
As I say yes to God,
Come into my life, do what You will.
His genes are and become mine,
I take on His very character
I am a son of God.
It was God's wish
To have many Sons.

Jesus grew in Mary's womb
But greater is the miracle for me,
Begotten by the Word,
He grows in my very being,
His life His character revealed in Me,
I'm now the temple of the living God
Becoming His hands, His feet,
His heart, as He grows in me
God's message to the world.
Yet I am not annihilated
I become myself, a son of God

Ready for eternity with Father.
It is God's wish
To have many Sons.

We are called, like Mary,
To bear the life of the Son of God . . .
Be his heart, His hands, His feet,
So God can show His character
To a lost unloving world.
Those who offer their lives
A living sacrifice
To bear His life, His word
Of life to others
Find their true destiny.
It is God's wish
To have many Sons.

Note

1 Jane Clark lives in Norway and has recently begun to write poetry embodying personal reflections on the Christian faith. This poem is reproduced in full with her permission.

11
The Mystery Called Prayer

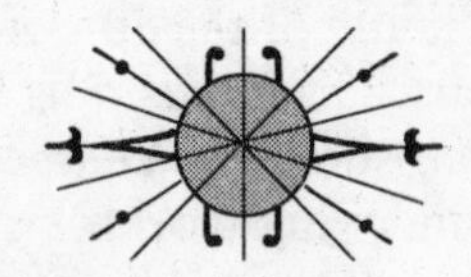

We have seen that, though our sins separate us from God, new birth in Christ can enable us to re-enter his presence and to be part of his family.

If you are a serious follower of Jesus and have put your trust in him as Saviour and Lord, then, even if this is not the sort of language with which you are normally comfortable, *you are a born-again Christian*. But you may well ask, 'If this is true, and if I may claim new birth in Christ, then how is it that I feel so inadequate and so vulnerable?'

The answer is that this is precisely how new-born babies do feel. The new arrivals in a maternity ward are weak and struggling beings. They need sustenance. They need help. They have a lot of growing ahead of them.

And that is exactly how it is with us. We are fragile and immature creatures, and even after accepting God's new life we need a great deal of help in order to grow and develop.

Fortunately aids to growth are generously available. The traditional theological term for them is 'means of grace'. It is, for instance, the nature of both sacraments and Scripture to serve as means of grace. In the prologue to this book we saw that to spiritual flatlanders the bread and wine of Holy Communion and the ancient words of Scripture seem out of date and irrelevant. Yet for those who are beginning to see the possibility of multidimensional living, experience shows that these are means by which sustenance and strength can be received for the Christian life.

The journey of prayer

The same is true of the mystery called prayer.

We do not always see prayer as a mystery. This is perhaps because it is such a common experience. If I were to ask you whether you had any personal experience of – say – the mystery of angels (see Chapter 2) or of perceiving God's Shekinah (see Chapter 9), the odds are that your answer would be 'No'. But prayer is different.

Jesus assumed that all his disciples would pray. 'When you pray, say "Our Father,"' he taught them. Note '*when*' not '*if*'.

Over many years of pastoral ministry I have learned that the vast majority of people do pray, even if only occasionally.

But we must not fall into the trap of supposing that because prayer is not rare, it therefore cannot be a mystery. It is part of the art of living to perceive the wondrous within the commonplace. The sunsets we see from our sitting-room window, with its views across the Irish sea to Snowdonia, are not rare, but Eira and I find them breathtakingly wonderful. We have a lot of roses in our little garden, but the fact that there are many of them does not make each one of them less of a wonder. The same is true of the human body and the human brain – and the human capacity for prayer.

So what is this process called prayer and how does it help us forward in our journey into mystery?

The *Encyclopaedia Britannica* defines prayer as 'man's personal directing of himself toward and intercourse with the transcendental reality'. Every religion interprets this process in a different way. For Christians, because Jesus has taught us that we have the privilege of calling God 'Father', the distinctive thing about prayer is that it is simply Life with Father.

Traditionally our communication with God the Father in prayer has been thought to involve four main elements. I was taught them as a teenager and have always been able to remember them easily, because when we take the first letter of each element, together they spell out the word ACTS.

Adoration

The first element is *Adoration*, which means practising the presence of God and in doing so both recognizing and responding to the mystery of his revealed nature. The psalmist records God's invitation to us, 'Be still, and know that I am God' (Psalm 46.10). Adoration is the mode of prayer which says 'Yes' to that invitation.

We may not find it easy to achieve a spirit of instant adoration in our daily prayer-time. Usually we need some sort of starter to focus our minds on God. Fortunately there are many of them available. We may have a favourite passage of Scripture which leads us into God's presence. Psalm 103 generally works for me, either in a traditional or modern translation of the Bible, or in the lovely hymn which is based on that psalm by Francis Henry Lyte, 'Praise, my soul, the King of Heaven'. Or there is the vision of heaven in Chapter 4 of the Revelation of St John the Divine, which is the basis of the magisterial hymn by Bishop Reginald Heber (1783–1826) which begins,

> Holy, Holy, Holy, Lord God almighty!
> Early in the morning our song shall rise to Thee;
> Holy, Holy, Holy, merciful and mighty,
> God in three persons, blessed Trinity.
> Holy, Holy, Holy! All the saints adore Thee,
> Casting down their golden crowns around the
> glassy sea;

Cherubim and Seraphim falling down before Thee,
Who wast and art and ever more shall be.

Alternatively, as you have probably guessed from my words above, I find that when I look across the sea towards Snowdonia, nature itself can take me into the presence of God and into a spirit of adoration.

I have written about adoration at greater length elsewhere, and will not repeat here the three prayer methods which are contained in *How to Pray when Life Hurts*, which many tell me help them to adore God, or the hints on learning to praise God which are contained at the end of that book (Lawrence, 1993, pp. 69–77).

But let me reiterate that the spirit of adoration is the heart of prayer. Until we can come into God's presence and marvel as we experience some degree of awareness of his nature and his will, nothing else will follow.

Confession

However, hard on the heels of a prayer of adoration will come prayer's second ingredient – *Confession*. For having looked at God, we find he then enables us to look at ourselves. We tend to think of confession in terms of acknowledging our sins, offering God our penitence, and asking for his forgiveness. These things are indeed a major element in confession. There is an aid to penitence at the end of Chapter 7 in this book and several more in *How to Pray when Life Hurts* (Lawrence, 1993, pp. 13–21).

You may like to pause for a moment and read Jesus' story about the Pharisee and the tax-collector praying in the Temple (Luke 18.9–14), which graphically illustrates his teaching that without penitence prayer is both unreal and ineffective.

But there is more to confession than penitence. Confession is owning up to *all* that is in us. Because we are sinners, the admission of sin will always have a major part in it, but confession does not end there. In prayer we are meant to admit not only that we are guilty and ashamed, but also perhaps that we are angry and depressed, anxious and fearful, stressed and tense, confused and bewildered, and much more besides. We are meant to take the whole bumper bundle of our nature and lay it before God without deception.

Confession means saying, 'Lord, when I look at you, I am moved to adoration, but when I look at myself, I have very different feelings. For you help me to see myself as I am, Lord, warts and all. And I know that if I do not come to you "just as I am" then I do not come in any real sense at all. So here I am, Lord. This is me – I confess it.'

This sort of prayer is very important, because though God can do nothing with pseudo-piety, he can do wonders when we come to him in naked honesty. It is not a pleasant form of prayer. Fortunately we are not required to wallow in it and soon we will find that we are being led out of confession into the third ingredient in prayer, which is *Thanksgiving*.

Thanksgiving

In contrast to confession, thanksgiving is a distinctly enjoyable form of prayer. Yet strangely most of us are not very good at it. So perhaps a little help would not come amiss at this point.

May I offer you what I like to call my 'Little and Large' formula for thanking God?

This method begins with the little things of life, as you let your mind wander over recent experiences. Think of people you have met during the last day or two, and of things you have done, and of situations you have encountered. As in your mind you relive each happening, watch out for the good experiences. As you remember the things which gave you joy, turn each one into a small prayer of thanksgiving. 'Thank you, God, for the postman's friendly smile.' 'Thank you for the lovely display of flowers in the park.' 'Thank you for the convenience of the local corner-shop.' 'Thank you for the postcard from friends on holiday.'

Then gradually allow the scope of your thanks to widen. List your physical blessings. Thank God for the parts of your body that are working well. It will make a change from fussing about any that are not. Be aware of your material blessings – your home, your food, your clothes, your warm bed, etc.

Then go beyond material things. Thank God for the relationships you value most – your parents, your children, your husband, your wife, your wider family, your circle of friends. Identify reasons for gratitude in your neighbourhood, in your work; in your leisure, in your life-style as a whole.

Finally let your thankfulness focus on the really large things – the beauty of nature, whatever inspires you in the world of music and literature and art, the gift of freedom, the awesomeness of the universe, and crowning everything the love of God, revealed in Christ.

Then – and only then – move to the final element in prayer, that of *Supplication* (or asking for things), which in its turn will subdivide into intercession (prayer for others) and petition (prayer for yourself).

Supplication

Here, as elsewhere, simple aids to prayer are not to be despised, such as, for example, the childlike practice of praying on the fingers of one hand. The thumb is nearest to us and reminds us to pray for those who are near and dear, listing their needs and sharing our hopes for them. The index finger is the teaching finger (try pointing or wagging any other one!) and reminds us to pray for teachers, preachers, writers, broadcasters and all who guide society in any way. The third finger is the tallest one and reminds us to pray for VIPs, the leaders of the nations, our own Queen and Prime Minister, all Members of Parliament, those involved in local government, and so on. The fourth finger is the weakest one and reminds us to pray for those who are in need – the sick, the hungry, the underprivileged, world-wide victims of violence or natural disaster. Finally our little finger helps us to have a sense of proportion as we pray for ourselves.

And what of the word ACTS itself? For it is certainly not without significance that this is what *A*doration, *C*onfession, *T*hanksgiving and *S*upplication together spell out.

To pray means to act

True prayer always leads to action. If you ever find yourself saying 'I'll pray about this or that' as a substitute for doing what you can, then beware! Such prayer is a travesty.

Occasionally I write little jingles about Christian life. I find that sometimes they have a 'Heineken effect'. They reach people and parts that would be inaccessible otherwise. One of them deals with the pointlessness of prayer without action. It starts with a couple of verses that go like this:

Uncle Willy was religious for the best part of his life,
But his prayer wasn't worth very much.
His conceit was quite prodigious and he used to beat his wife!
So his prayer wasn't worth very much.

Cousin Chloe was quite clear in condemning every sin,
But her prayer wasn't worth very much.

When a friend in need was near, she'd pretend she wasn't in,
So her prayer wasn't worth very much.

Each verse is followed by this chorus:

For unless our prayer is just a pose
We can't put it off with our Sunday clothes,
But into our life with power it goes –
or our prayer isn't worth very much!

Monks of old might well have echoed the same thought. In their life they aimed both to pray (*orare*) and to work (*laborare*), and they regarded the two as one. As we saw earlier, Christianity is a 'so-what?' religion. The gospel always has consequences – and so has prayer.

However, why should all of this have a place in a book about mystery? Thanking God for the corner-shop and asking him to guide our MP and doing whatever we can to improve the world after giving ourselves a good talking-to in prayer – these things clearly have their place in Christian life. But are they not a touch commonplace? Where is the mystery in such prayer?

Prayer as a relationship

It lies not so much in our approach to God as in his response to us. For prayer is a two-way process, not a monologue but a conversation, not a recital but a relationship.

So consider now the four ingredients of prayer from the viewpoint of God's dealings with us, God's friendship with us, God's communion with the depths of our being.

When we offer God our first hesitant and tentative prayer of *Adoration*, he responds by enlarging and improving our capacity for this sort of prayer. He shows us more of himself and in doing so helps us to discover not only his nature but our own too. For we were created in order to glorify him.

The Christian faith is full of paradoxes. One of them is the fact that to glorify ourselves is to shrink and die, whereas to glorify God is to live and grow. It is not till we are 'lost in wonder, love and praise' that we can know that we have been truly found by the God of Love. As we adore his unique and perfect Love, that Love affirms us and we realize we are precious in his sight. It is only as we bow low before our Creator that we find we are able to walk tall as his creatures.

And with that realization comes a new ability to be honest to God, a new and more courageous capacity for *Confession.*

As in the case of adoration, the prayer of confession is a dialogue, a two-way process. When we confess our sins and ask for forgiveness in the name of Jesus, we discover the God who likes to say 'Yes'. The sins that should separate us from him lose their power to do so. For God's costly and mysterious gospel of redemption has greater power than they do.

This gospel also ministers to us in every other aspect of life, whenever we are moved to be honest about ourselves to God.

If the state of mind which we are led to share with him is one of anger or of a depression that has suppressed anger at its roots, then we are privileged, in the memorable words of Archbishop Robert Leighton, to 'vent our rage into the bosom of God'. We are mysteriously allowed to approach the crucified Lord and let our rage loose on him. If there is anger in you now (and anger is a very common element within ordinary human nature, whether we are aware of it or not), then you are actually permitted to hammer the nails into the hands of Jesus and ram the crown of thorns onto his brow. As we saw in Chapter 8, the strange mission of the Son of God is that of dying at our hands, but then of rising again, still loving us. That dying and risen love is just as effective in quelling the destructive power of our anger as it is in preventing our sins from separating us from God. I have written in much greater detail about this in *How to Pray when Life Hurts* (Lawrence, 1993, pp. 23–31).

In the same book (pp. 43–50) there are details of the way in which he also brings us healing if it is a spirit of fearfulness which we must bring to him, whether we experience it as a low-level anxiety or as a soul-threatening sense of dereliction. For he meets us at the very heart of mental anguish. Though Jesus is God, yet by a dark miracle he has experienced what it means to feel God-forsaken (Mark 15.34). It is part of the mystery of the gospel that there is a real sense in which we have to stoop to meet God. For no matter how low life may bring us, God comes to us from below. If it should be that you and I have to enter into the deep pain of inner fearfulness, however deeply we may go, Christ will have always penetrated more deeply. He offers himself as our companion on the way, our guide, our fellow-sufferer. This sacrificial and healing companionship is, I believe, the most precious gift in the world. It may even be that within eternity those who have known the deepest fearfulness in the company of Jesus will be regarded as the most fortunate of all. For they will know aspects of his nature and of his healing power of which others must remain ignorant.

Whatever it may be that we find ourselves bringing to God out of our experience of life, as we learn more of the principles and practice of confessional prayer, we will discover that within the gospel there are healing resources to meet us at every point of need. So it is that confession leads naturally to *Thanksgiving*.

As we offer our thankfulness to God, he responds by

increasing our capacity for thanksgiving. We see that there is more and more in life for which the only proper response is gratitude. I love the grace, 'O God, who hast given us so much, give us yet one thing more – a thankful heart for Jesus' sake.' It is a prayer well worth praying, for with every increase in our level of gratitude there comes a new sense of joy and liberation. To be thankful is to have our feet set in a large room. It is to become a citizen of the universe. It is also, amazingly, a way of giving joy to God. For God is thankful for our thankfulness.

Set, as we are, in a world which is so often spoiled by human sinfulness, a world of need and trouble, we shall find ourselves passing naturally from prayers of thankfulness to acts of *Supplication*.

God wants us to share with him all that we think and feel. So it is his will that we share such perception as we may have of the way in which the world in general and our own little personal sphere in particular could become better places.

We are assured that these supplicatory prayers will make a difference. For God has mysteriously limited himself by offering us the generous but hazardous gift of free will. Our misuse of free will means that there is much of his own will which is obstructed. When we truly offer supplicatory prayer in the name of Jesus, what we do is to place part of our free will at God's disposal, as we align our mind with his mind.

What then is his response as we do so? In a word, when we make a request in the name of Jesus, God answers it. Scripture guarantees this again and again.

But does he?

When prayer seems unanswered

We come here to one of the great enigmas of ordinary Christian experience. Why is it that though most of us could provide examples of answered prayer from our own experience, we can usually also tell of prayers which seem not to have been answered?

Matilda comes to mind. When she was a comparatively new Christian, she told me that she believed she had a special talent for prayer. She felt she had real influence with God. Her prayers 'worked'. Everything she asked for she got. She testified to it at church meetings.

Then everything changed. Nothing seemed to work for her in prayer. She was confused about this and rather angry. She felt betrayed. She stopped coming to church and there was nothing I could say or do to bring her back again. Now, years later, she is still a non-churchgoer.

What are we to make of Matilda's experience?

It is a fact of life that when we make a request in prayer, God sometimes seems to say 'Yes', sometimes 'No', and sometimes 'Wait'. But knowing that this is what happens is not the same as understanding why.

Maybe our limited minds are not capable of discovering an explanation. Perhaps we ought to have the wisdom just to acknowledge a mystery here and to say with Job that there are 'things too wonderful for me to know' (Job 42.3).

And yet at the risk of rushing in where angels fear to tread, let me try to offer one or two fallible thoughts. They are bound to be inadequate, but they may possibly serve as a stimulus for deeper and better reflection subsequently.

Three stages in the life of prayer

I believe there are three stages to be experienced in prayer-life. The first one, which characterizes our early days as Christians, consists of a rather wheedling attempt to get God on our side in the game of life, a childish desire to persuade God to help us have our own way. It is almost as though we climb up on Father's knee and plead that he will grant us a favour. The remarkable thing is that often at this stage he seems to oblige. We seek to manipulate God and for a while he lets us get away with it.

But of course it would not be good for us if we were permitted to remain fixated at this stage. Sooner or later God must show us that Christian prayer is not just a means of getting our own way. We have to be taught to place God's will above our own, to say 'Thy will be done' and to mean it. And so there comes a second stage in prayer (and it may be a long one) during which we learn from experience that when we bring our shopping-list to God, it will be returned with some of the items crossed out. For reasons which we may or may not understand they do not fall within his will.

However, for some people at any rate, there is a third stage in prayer, during which, because we have become more aware of and more committed to God's will, we are once again enabled to make specific requests in the name of Jesus and to find that we have a new prayer-power as we do so.

In this sequence the first and third stages may superficially seem similar, but in fact they could not be further apart. Let me offer two illustrations to make the point.

In my early and distinctly immature days as a Christian, I had a considerable yen for a commission in the Territorial Army. However, I faced a problem in this which seemed insuperable. In order to be recommended by a selection board, candidates had to pass various tests. One of them was to climb a rope. This was something I had never been able to do.

As my first attempt at a selection board had ended in failure and this was one of the reasons, I took the matter to the Lord in prayer. I think I knew that it was a totally selfish prayer, but nonetheless I asked God somehow so to influence the situation that I would pass my next selection board in spite of my deficiency in the rope-climbing department. He did just that. In due course I was summoned to a second selection board and on this occasion, to my immense gratification, just before the rope-climbing test I was called away from the rest of the group for an individual interview, and by the time I returned the programme had moved on and I had been credited with passing the test even though I had not taken it. So it was that I was commissioned.

I had the grace to be awed by this demonstration of the power of God, but it certainly marked me out as having progressed no further than stage one in my prayers at that time in my life.

By contrast, consider this story told me by Aubrey, a man of action whose eventful life included a period as a fighter-pilot in the Second World War. He was shot down over France and was found by some nuns who hid him in their convent and cared for him. He needed a good deal of care because for a while he was injured and delirious. His main recollection of this time of illness is the curious one of remembering the sausages he used to enjoy eating at home, and ultimately it was the smell of sizzling sausages which brought him back to consciousness. One of the nuns subsequently told him that in the midst of his delirium he had been asking for sausages. There was not a sausage in the convent, but, seeing that this was important to him, the nuns went into their chapel and asked God for sausages. Next morning they found a parcel of sausages on their front doorstep!

This was stage three praying and is a totally different phenomenon from my rope-climbing escapade. Aubrey was a different man afterwards physically, mentally and spiritually. Those sausages had honoured God and advanced his kingdom.

You will, of course, see all sorts of flaws in my theory of the three stages of prayer. I can see them myself.

For instance, though I am firmly committed to the ministry of Christian healing, and though I have been privileged to see miracles taking place within this ministry, there have been other occasions when after faithful prayer in the name of Jesus (stage three prayer, one would have thought) the discernible results seemed negligible. I have attempted to write in a balanced way both about the wonders and the problems of this ministry in *The Practice of Christian Healing* (Lawrence, 1998).

Also, though I believe I can perceive three prayer stages in theory, they are far from distinct or clear-cut in practice. At this moment, for instance, in your own prayer life you may find yourself somewhere between stage one and two or between stages two and three. You may even find yourself experiencing all three stages, commuting from one to another, as life's circumstances and your own reactions vary. Jesus would understand this, for even he had to resist the lure of stage one praying, when he was urged by the devil to use his spiritual influence to turn stones into bread during his time of temptation in the wilderness (Matthew 4.3–4), and though his healing ministry was based on stage three prayer, yet he was forced back into stage two prayer before the crucifixion, as he hoped against hope that he would not be required by his Father to drain the impending cup of suffering, but added, 'Yet not what I will, but what you will' (Mark 14.36).

Spiritual exercise

What we have been doing is scratching the surface of the mystery of prayer – and what I would suggest is that now it is time to stop the scratching and to turn to prayer itself.

So as the spiritual exercise at the end of this chapter, why not give yourself slowly and expectantly to the four elements of Adoration, Confession, Thanksgiving and Supplication, considering, as you do so, where next they are pointing you in your Christian adventure, your journey into mystery.

Though this has been a longish chapter, it is vital to know that praying is more important than writing about it or reading about it. For whether our prayers are primitive or advanced, ignorant or informed, childish or mature in Christ, we still need them. They are like the breathing equipment used by a deep-sea diver or a Himalayan mountaineer. Without them we have no hope of plumbing the depths or scaling the heights.

And a final thought, one that is as mind-numbing as any of the mysteries that we have yet considered in this book. It is a basic Christian conviction that prayer not only spells out ACTS on our part, but on God's part too. Prayer channels God's redemptive and recreative will. Prayer hastens God's kingdom. Prayer removes the shackles which God allows the misuse of our freedom to place upon his activity in the world. In other words, amazingly, incredibly, miraculously, your faltering prayer-life and mine somehow empowers the omnipotent God!

Epilogue

Mystery without End

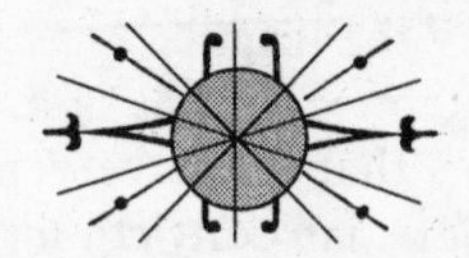

Jacob was anything but a natural religious leader. His story is told in the second half of the book of Genesis. The name Jacob means 'supplanter' and sounds rather like the Hebrew word for 'heel' and, if the truth is to be told, in his earlier days he behaved like a heel. 'Tricky Jake' would not be a bad version of his name.

He cheated his brother Esau, who was not very bright, out of the blessing which should have come to him as a birthright from his father. Esau hated him for it and vowed to kill him after their father's death (Genesis 27.41). So for his own protection his mother sent him away to live with his Uncle Laban, who was just as tricky as he was.

It was on his way there that Jacob had an extraordinary mystical experience. He stopped for the night at a rocky place in the hill-country to the north of Jerusalem, and there, as he slept,

> He dreamt that he saw a stairway reaching from earth to heaven, with angels going up and coming down on it. And there was the Lord standing beside him. 'I am the Lord, the God of Abraham and Isaac,' he said. 'I will give to you and to your descendants this land on which you are lying. They will be as numerous as the specks of

> dust on the earth. They will extend their territory in all directions, and through you and your descendants I will bless all the nations. Remember, I will be with you and protect you wherever you go, and I will bring you back to this land. I will not leave you until I have done all that I have promised you. (Genesis 28.12–15)

If you feel that Jacob was hardly the most worthy person to have the privilege of such a promise, you may also feel that his response to God left much to be desired. Tricksters tend to be 'iffy' people, and 'if' was the first word of his response. '*If* you will be with me and protect me on the journey I am making and give me food and clothing and *if* I return safely to my father's home, then you will be my God' (Genesis 28.20–21).

So began an uneasy and conditional relationship with God. It hardly had the nature of a trusting friendship. It was more like a wrestling match and was symbolized by a strange occasion when he found himself literally wrestling with a stranger, whom subsequently he came to think of as God himself (Genesis 32.22–32).

After the wrestling match Jacob was given a new name – no longer Jacob, Tricky Jake, Jake the heel, but 'Israel', a word which in Hebrew sounds like 'one who struggles with God' or 'one with whom God struggles'. From then on he walked with a limp, because the wrestling had damaged his hip – but he had moved forward spiritually and the new name was a sign of it.

The Bible tells us that he went on to have twelve sons, whose relationships were as turbulent as that of Jacob and Esau. Yet one of them, Joseph, was able to save both his father and the rest of the family when hard times came, by providing them with a home in Egypt, where he had become great and influential.

When the old 'God-struggler' died he was honoured by

Jews and Egyptians alike, and before his death he managed to accomplish what he had actually prevented his own father from doing. He bestowed a blessing of his choice upon each of his sons. The words can be found in Genesis, Chapter 49. If you read them, don't miss amongst them the one and only statement which at that stage he wanted to make about himself. It comes in verse 18 – 'I wait for your deliverance, Lord.'

Perhaps ultimately he was to be given a third name, not 'heel' or 'trickster', not 'God-struggler', but simply 'a man delivered by God'. But for that renaming he knew he had to wait, he had to ascend the eternal ladder which he had seen in his mysterious dream.

My hope and prayer is that this book may serve as a sort of 'Jacob's ladder', a fleeting glance at God's eternal light, a glimpse of his glory. If it should be so for you in any way, possibly you may find that your own response is as conditional as Jacob's was – 'Lord, if you do this, that and the other for me, then you will be my God.' We are frequently less than wholehearted in God's service. To be a Christian is often to be a 'God-struggler'.

If this is your own experience of Christian life, if you marvel at the mystery of God but find yourself struggling with him – be encouraged. Maybe it would do no harm to check the direction of your life once again, but if that check shows you that for all your shortcomings it *is* your will to move not towards the devil's engulfing darkness but towards God's irradiating light, then be encouraged. Carry on struggling, if you must, but carry on marvelling too, and know that by God's grace we can learn both to bear and share his light. Know also that in your journey into mystery there is much more to come. For God is infinite and you and I are called to explore his infinity. The name you bear now is a precious name. It was given to you in baptism and is known to God. But there is a new name awaiting you in the mystery of eternity, a name which signifies all that you are yet to become (Revelation 2.17). God bless you as your journey into that mystery continues. For the gospel promises that it is a mystery without end. And the best is yet to be.

Further Reading

Bainton, Roland H. (1955) *Here I Stand*, Abingdon Press.

Douglas-Smith, Basil (1983) *The Mystics Come to Harley Street*, Regency Press.

Howatch, Susan (1997) *A Question of Integrity*, Little, Brown & Co.

Joad, C. E. M. (1942) *God and Evil*, Faber & Faber.

Kendrick, Graham (1987) *Shine Jesus Shine*, Make Way Music.

Lake, Frank (1966) *Clinical Theology*, Darton, Longman & Todd.

Lawrence, Roy (1979) *Invitation to Healing*, Kingsway.

Lawrence, Roy (1993) *How to Pray when Life Hurts*, Scripture Union.

Lawrence, Roy (1996) *Make Me a Channel*, Scripture Union.

Lawrence, Roy (1997) *Christ with Us*, Scripture Union.

Lawrence, Roy (1998) *The Practice of Christian Healing*, Triangle.

Lewis, C. S. (1949) *Transposition and other Addresses*, Geoffrey Bles.

Mayne, Michael (1995) *This Sunrise of Wonder*, Fount.

Moody, Raymond (1976) *Life after Life*, Bantam.

Peddie, J. Cameron (1966) *The Forgotten Talent*, Fontana.

Rawlings, Maurice (1979) *Beyond Death's Door*, Sheldon Press.

Ritchie, George (1978) *Return from Tomorrow*, Kingsway.

Roose-Evans, James (1998) *Inner Journey, Outer Journey*, Darton, Longman & Todd.